MACMILLAN CARIBBEAN WRITERS

Two Can Play

with

School's Out

and

The Power

Trevor D Rhone

MACMILLAN
CARIBBEAN

Macmillan Education
Macmillan Building
4 Crinan Street
Islington
London
N1 9XW
A division of Macmillan Publishers Limited
Companies and representatives throughout the world

www.macmillan-caribbean.com

ISBN: 978-1-4050-5746-2

Typeset by EXPO Holdings
Cover design by John Barker
Cover photographs by Monica daSilva

Printed and bound in China

2018 2017 2016
10 9 8 7 6

Macmillan Caribbean Writers Series

Trevor Rhone's Jamaican comedies, which have featured in film, on television and radio as well as in theatre, are admired for their authenticity in every aspect, from language to character to challenges common in West Indian life. Rhone's enduring popularity reflects not only his gift for comic dialogue that sounds as natural as a conversation at a bus stop, but also his ability to make us look again, from an uncompromising angle, wherever rethinking and reform could make our world a better place. This new collection contains two of his most successful plays, *Two Can Play* and *School's Out*. Also included is *The Power*, a BBC-commissioned radio play published here for the first time.

The Macmillan Caribbean Writers Series (MCW) is an exciting new library of fine writing which treats the broad range of the Caribbean experience. As well as play collections, which include the Gayelle series, selected as particularly suitable for arts and drama festivals, MCW offers a wide choice of novels, novellas and short stories, by both new and established writers, and also embraces works of poetry and non-fiction. Writers on the list come from around the region, including Guyana, Trinidad, Tobago, Barbados, St Vincent, Bequia, Grenada, St Lucia, Dominica, Montserrat, Antigua, the Bahamas, Jamaica and Belize.

MCW was launched in 2003 at the Caribbean's premier literary event, the Calabash Festival in Jamaica. Macmillan Caribbean is also proud to be associated with the work of the Cropper Foundation in Trinidad, developing the talents of the region's most promising emerging writers, many of whom are contributors to MCW.

Judy Stone
Series Editor
Macmillan Caribbean Writers

Contents

Introduction

Pa Trevor

"Pa Ben ready! Run come! Story time!"
Trevor Rhone: *Old Story Time*

In 1971, a struggling thirty-year-old playwright of, till then, modest achievement but indomitable spirit, hit the Jamaican jackpot. *Smile Orange* was not only the most successful theatrical production Kingston had ever seen, it ignited an unquenchable passion, amongst both the Caribbean public and the region's arts critics, for the West Indian comedies of Trevor Rhone. Before he was fifty, Rhone was being described as "the father of Jamaican Theatre".

Truthfully, there were many fathers and mothers of Caribbean Theatre before Rhone. The early twentieth century saw a blossoming of pioneering playwrights throughout the West Indies, most spectacularly in Jamaica, Guyana and Trinidad. Vera Bell, Kate Bourne, Norman Cameron, Mabel Caudeiron, Esme Cendrecourt, Sam Chase, Ernest Cupidon, Philip Gaines, Marcus Garvey, Errol Hill, Frank Hill, C L R James, Errol John, Archie Lindo, Roger Mais, Una Marson, Sidney Martin, W G Ogilvie, Tom Redcam, Eric Roach, Arthur Roberts, DeWilton Rogers, Cicely Waite-Smith, Derek and Roderick Walcott and Ranny Williams are some of the better-known names engraved on the roll call of those who, each in his or her own way, sought to play their part in the development of a West Indian Theatre.

Certain basic elements were common to many of the early works for the West Indian stage. There seemed to be an instinctive consensus that the regional theatre needed plays with settings recognisably within the region, cast with characters recognisably of the region, speaking from a regional viewpoint in a recognisably regional voice, and dealing with specifically regional situations.

Some playwrights incorporated just one or two of these elements, many incorporated most or all of them. Some crafted the elements more effectively than others. But it was Rhone who first achieved a balance of all the elements so felicitous, so funny, so frankly Jamaican that his fellow West Indians responded in numbers and with a joyous enthusiasm never seen before.

It was his frankness that served Rhone so well, along with his sense of humour and his ear for authentic dialogue. His settings were not only everyday Jamaican settings, he made no attempt to prettify the unlovely, and this honesty resonated with his audiences. His characters were equally frankly drawn. Whereas Derek Walcott, for instance, would elevate even his humblest characters to a level of grandeur, Rhone stripped his of pretension, exposing all too familiar Caribbean warts and weaknesses. And he was fearless in tackling uncomfortable, often unspoken themes of racism, machismo, incompetence, bullying and women's rights. But whereas Errol John and others treated social concerns as high drama, Rhone did his campaigning through comedy.

With play after play of his a box-office triumph, Rhone has tapped into a particular vein of popular theatre that uses laughter as the language of social commentary. His predecessors in world theatre range from the still-produced Aristophanes of four centuries before Christ, to the 1997 Nobel Laureate, Italian political activist Darius Fo. In West Indian theatre it is less easy to pinpoint Rhone's predecessors. During the first half of the twentieth century the most successful such blend of belly-laughter and social commentary was probably that found in the calypso tents. In the region's more formal theatre, still in the early stages of its development out of the nationalist movement, for the most part comedy was farce, tragedy was heroic, and social concerns were serious business.

The realist literature of the nationalist movement, in such novels as C L R James's *Minty Alley* and Roger Mais's *The Hills Were Joyful Together*, incorporated a certain bitter-sweet humour that flowered naturally in the situations of rank poverty that were the settings of these works. With the transfer of the nationalist themes to the stage in the nineteen-fifties and sixties, in the yard plays of Douglas Archibald and others, the humour intensified and became less cynical. The finest yard play ever written, Errol John's *Moon on a Rainbow Shawl*, is leavened with ribaldry, mockery and gentle mirth. But the essential character of *Moon* is more sombre, weighted with a wrenching interweaving of passion and rejection, dreams and nightmares, violence and disappointment. It is not non-stop, roll-in-the-aisles comedy, which Rhone's work often is, for all the gravity of his themes.

But Rhone's comedy is not crudely bawdy as, say, Aristophanes can be, and as the raucously popular Jamaican 'crotch' theatre always is. Euphemisms, suggestiveness and double-entendres notwithstanding, you could safely take your maiden aunt to a Rhone play, knowing that she will roll comfortably in the aisles with you. Another aspect of Rhone's comedy is that it lacks malice. His endearing affection for all his characters, his charitable understanding of their human failings and foibles, contribute hugely to their appeal.

Before *Smile Orange*, with its inside look at a tourist hotel staffed by smartmen and chupidees, Jamaicans had never seen themselves represented on stage with such realism. They couldn't get enough of the experience. They flocked in such numbers to Kingston's small Barn Theatre, where Rhone was resident playwright, that whereas previously most Jamaican producers could have counted the days of their production run on their fingers, Rhone's first big hit ran for a record-annihilating 245 performances.

By the early twenty-first century, out of an oeuvre of more than twenty works for stage, screen, television and radio, Rhone's greatest successes included, as well as *Smile Orange*, both the stage play, which in 1972 represented Jamaica at the inaugural Carifesta in Guyana, and the equally popular award-winning film (1974), which Rhone directed himself, the plays *The Gadget*, which won the 1969 Jamaica Arts Festival silver medal, *Blue Socks Blues* (1970 JAF bronze), *School's Out* (1974), *Old Story Time* (1979), *Two Can Play* (1982 Best Jamaican Play), which was produced for Kentucky television, *Bellas Gate Boy* (2002) and the films *The Harder They Come* (co-authored 1969) and *Milk and Honey* (1988), which won the Toronto Film Festival Genie Award for Best Original Screenplay.

These dramatic achievements are all the more impressive for the sheer unlikelihood, as he was growing up, that the young Rhone could ever have realised his childhood ambition of making a career for himself in theatre. For a start, at the time there was no full-time professional theatre in Jamaica. Even if there had been, the playwright's first efforts as an amateur actor betrayed a vast ignorance of the craft and an apparent unsuitability for its pursuit. And, as the twenty-first and last-born in his penny-poor rural family, with all the competing needs of his twenty siblings, he could not expect any financial support to enable him to go overseas to study at drama school and improve his prospects.

As Rhone recounts in *Bellas Gate Boy*, his hilarious autobiographical monologue, his determination was undimmed by such overwhelming odds. Somehow he managed to gain entrance to a British drama school, the Rose Bruford College in London. Somehow, with his mother's help, a skeleton purse was put together to get him there. Once there, he somehow managed to survive, to learn, and eventually to shine. But there were no roles for him in England, and on his return to theatre-poor Jamaica he had to create both his own physical stage in a Kingston garage and, eventually, his own repertoire of plays.

When he first began to write for Jamaican audiences, Rhone had convinced himself that he should write in standard English. Even after the success of his 1967 vernacular poem *Look Two* – a simple but absurdly entertaining conversation at a bus stop – Rhone had hesitated to write his plays in the vernacular, anticipating that he would then lose access to the international market. *Smile Orange* was the first play in which he took the plunge into vernacular dialogue, with unprecedentedly successful results.

As commentator Mervyn Morris later pointed out, writing *Smile Orange* in the vernacular was not the risk Rhone had feared. *"The way had been prepared by – for example – Louise Bennett in her dialect writings and performance, by the LTM pantomime as it evolved, by comedians Bim and Bam in their topical stage shows, by a popular radio serial scripted by Elaine Perkins."* [1]

Several of Rhone's plays have been published over the years, but this new Macmillan Caribbean Writers Series collection of three of his works includes *The Power*, which has never previously appeared in print, as well as two of his most frequently produced comedies. *Two Can Play* is perhaps the finest example to date of the playwright's skill in crafting natural Jamaican speech. *School's Out*, however, is a remarkable exercise in character-driven speech, with variations from expatriate English and educated Jamaican to vernacular used as protest and standard English mauled by ignorance. Despite its rural setting *The Power*, written for the BBC, reverts to so close an approximation of standard English that it serves to highlight the immense contribution Rhone's use of the vernacular has made to the success of his stage plays.

---

[1] Mervyn Morris, Critical Introduction, *Old Story Time and Smile Orange*, Longman 1981

The format of Rhone's 1982 Best Jamaican Play *Two Can Play* is unusual in Rhone's oeuvre, and indeed in West Indian theatre generally, for it is a two-hander. Since Edward Albee's 1958 milestone *The Zoo Story*, two-handers have become increasingly popular in western theatre – popular with the producers who find them economical and relatively easy to stage, with the actors who find them a rewarding challenge, and with audiences who appreciate a deeper and more intimate involvement with the characters. West Indian theatre, however, still generally leans towards larger casts, and in genres such as folk theatre, very large casts indeed. The few successful two-handers from the region include Walcott's *Pantomime*, Mustapha Matura's *Rum an' Coca-Cola*, Patrick Brown's *December* and plays by Lennox Brown, most of which have been produced outside the Caribbean.

The first Jamaican production of *Two Can Play* toured in the Caribbean and Canada, and other productions quickly followed, in London, New York, and in Paris as *Jeu pour Deux*. A taped version was screened in America by Kentucky Education Television.

The play is set in the late seventies, a time when Kingston was ravaged by political violence, and opens with a gun battle raging outside a downtown bedroom window. It is because of the fighting that Jim and Gloria, the occupants of that bedroom, have smuggled their three children to what they believe will be a better life in America. The parents have had to remain in Jamaica to care for Jim's dying father, Pops, one of the many off-stage characters who, as in *Smile Orange* and to a lesser extent *School's Out*, enliven the on-stage action. Jim, guarding against his offspring's possible discovery and deportation by the US immigration authorities, has insisted there be no communication between the two generations until the children have managed to establish legal residence in the States. Gloria, while apparently

...at, has shrewdly worked out a code that keeps ...ith her children at minimal risk, so that she knows ...o find them when Pops's death releases the pair.

Jim, for most of the play, as he has done for the twenty years of his marriage, does a great deal of insisting. Insisting is for him proof of his status as the typical macho West Indian male. He is adept at twisting situations to suit himself, and so is unfazed by the frequency with which his decisions, often the result of overreaction and panic, prove to have been unconsidered or simply foolish. He is unconscious of any irony in his assumption of superiority, even though his behaviour reeks of dishonesty, selfishness, cowardice, greed, laziness, prejudice and unfaithfulness. He insists that Gloria, rather than he, should run the gauntlet of the guns to get his father's medicine. He insists that Gloria, rather than he, should take the risks involved in their devious scheme to acquire US citizenship by taking flight for America and marrying there. He insists that Gloria, rather than he, should clean up his three-week-old squalor and cook for him the minute she walks into the house on her return to Jamaica.

For twenty years Gloria, who of the pair has the better brains, the greater courage, common sense and resourcefulness, has accepted her role as Jim's doormat. Accustomed as she is to having continually to rescue her husband from the consequences of his bungling boorishness, it is not until the catalyst of the trip to America that she recognises her own self-worth, and accepts her right to life as an individual.

Gloria and Jim are two of the most acutely drawn characters Rhone has yet created. And while in the first act, leading up to the trip, the play seems to be essentially a comedy on the time-honoured theme of escape to the promised land, the second act, in which Gloria returns as the wife of an American, establishes the play as primarily a character study, with the plot being almost as incidental as the shooting. As Jamaica's former Prime Minister Michael Manley wrote in his foreword to the play:

> "Two Can Play *is about love, and estrangement; about domination, and liberation; about confusion, and compassion. It is about two human beings who nearly lose one another - but who eventually struggle back together through uncertainty, through quarrels, through humiliation. Ultimately, Gloria and Jim survive because they learn to communicate and, finally, to re-discover one another - not so much as they were, but as what they each can try to become."* [2]

While the play itself is engagingly Jamaican in every detail, especially its humour, the subjugation of women is a subject both age-old and universal. Manley believes that Rhone's treatment, particularly in its moving resolution, elevates the writer "above the status of a good, or even brilliant, playwright - and suggests that he may indeed be a great one."

To Morris, "*Gloria and Jim can also function as metaphors for contending (political) forces in Jamaica.*"[3] Many Jamaicans migrated to the States in the seventies but, as Gloria says, "*America won't solve we problems, whether we go or whether we stay, until we start to look into weself an' learn to help each other.*" Though the US theme is secondary, it is of particular interest in that *Two Can Play* is one of the first regional works to reverse the popular thrust to emigration for self-betterment, by suggesting, in the end, that the West Indian is better off staying in the West Indies.

The second play in this collection, *School's Out*, although one of Rhone's most relentlessly funny, is the least optimistic in

---

[2] Michael Manley, Foreword, *Two Can Play*, Longman 1986

[3] Mervyn Morris, Critical Introduction, *Two Can Play*, Longman 1986

outlook. It suggests that there may be no hope for Jamaica's educational system. Warmed though they must be by convulsive laughter throughout the performance, concerned members of the audience will leave the theatre chilled to have seen how easily goodwill, good intentions and the will to reform can be crushed under the collective heel of indiscipline, jealousy, idleness, malicious rumour, ignorance, fear of challenge and fear of change to the status quo, however uncomfortable.

Set in a run-down Jamaican school, the comedy is based on Rhone's own experiences in the teaching profession. It has a medium-sized cast of seven, but as with *Smile Orange* it is an all-male cast apart from one actress. For the original production, which broke the *Smile Orange* box office record, Rhone himself created the lead role of Russ Dacres.

In this unnervingly believable horror story of school life in Jamaica, school is not 'out' in the sense of its being on holiday or after hours. The play is set on a school day in term time, but this particular church school is 'out' of all the essentials: materials, morals, manners, discipline, academic standards, an active headmaster, teachers who teach, plumbing that flushes. The audience has only a brief glimpse of one student, but offstage the directionless youngsters are running riot while the teachers largely ignore them from the shelter of the staffroom on stage. As in *Smile Orange*, which is set in the staff-only areas of a tourist hotel, Rhone presents the whole picture from the one side the public never sees, behind the scenes.

The various members of staff are too generously characterised to be stereotypes, but they are nevertheless universally familiar. Mr Josephs, the senior master and a product of outdated colonial education, is a failure who harps on about the old days. Young Hopal Hendry, the ill-educated and incompetent product of the new regime, develops during the play from being the butt of his colleagues' schoolboy jokes to being, frighteningly, the one most likely to succeed in his career. Pat Campbell is an expatriate with a thin skin and pretensions to superiority. Mica Adams, the female teacher, is well-intentioned but fickle. The Chaplain is unabashedly lecherous and idle. Rosco Callendar, who though little more admirable in his behaviour is the most sympathetic of this motley crew, resembles the hero of the Ti-Jean folk cycle in his swift understanding, sense of humour, private morality and refusal to exert himself unnecessarily.

Into this abysmal collection of misfits sweeps Russ Dacres, an idealistic new broom eager to set the school to rights, but lacking the diplomacy needed to scratch up the dust without choking himself. The play follows Russ's brief effort to turn the school into a genuine centre of learning, but the effort is doomed. A malfunctioning staff lavatory dominates both stage and dialogue, and in the end the triumphantly malfunctioning staff, by means of rumour and character assassination, transfers the symbolism of the stench from themselves, the staffroom, their school, and the whole educational system, to the decent and hardworking Russ.

Though most of the staff speak the standard English of the educated Jamaican, in *School's Out* Rhone introduces two interesting variations in his use of the vernacular. In the case of Hopal it is not the vernacular, his natural speech, which betrays Hopal's poverty of wits, it is the poverty of his grasp of standard English. Roscoe, intelligent and well-educated, speaks the vernacular as a form of protest against the system in which he finds himself enmeshed.

Critic Ken Jaikaransingh, who taught for a number of years in a leading Port of Spain boys' college, sees Rhone's landscape as extending even beyond the school system, to the far reaches of the emerging post-colonial society, much along the lines of the metaphor in Nigerian novelist Femi Osofisan's *Kolera Kolej*. Jaikaransingh writes:

"It needs little stretch of the imagination to place his [Rhone's] characters into types, and to see the staffroom as an abandoned Third World Nation, presided over, 'in absentia', by an invisible headmaster, represented now by the expatriate transient Patrick Campbell, and by the veteran Mr Josephs, whose regard for reputation and tradition has led him to adopt an alienated, uncommitted stance. The worst aspects of the colonial legacy are embodied in the chaplain, whose lechery, indolence and pettiness are masked by his clerical collar. Hopal Hendry is a bastard child of the colonial experience, conspicuously under-qualified to teach, yet earning tenure by ingratiating himself with the Head and acting as house-boy for the rest of the staff. Rosco Callendar cynically rejects the hypocrisies around him, but ironically capitalises on its weaknesses for his own benefit. He is, in a sense, the most culpable of them all, perceptive enough to recognise the waste around him but too selfish for any reaction other than buffoonery. Russ Dacres is the 'arriviste', full of new ideas, keen to make radical reforms, and undone eventually by his fellows, his own naïveté and by the uncompromising zeal of his crusade."[4]

The last play in this collection, *The Power*, is a radio play that was commissioned by BBC Radio 5, produced and broadcast in 1992. It is essentially a motivational tale for children, though its message can extend to adult audiences. It is a simple, straightforward story with few surprises and, for Rhone, a quite muted sense of comedy.

A father driving his young son to school tells him a story designed to encourage the son to achieve better results through greater self-confidence. The dramatised story is of two boys in

---

[4] Ken Jaikaransingh, *"School's Out", a dark alarming vision*, Daily Express 16 November 1988.

the same class at the rural village school of Look Behind. The boys are the school's two possible contenders for a scholarship that is the chance of a lifetime. Only one of them can sit the examination. The poorer of the two boys, Theophilus, who has to take days off school to help his mother with chores such as toting water from the river, is convinced that his rival Mark is innately more intelligent than he, and will win the chance to sit the scholarship. Mark is of similar mind, but to ensure his superiority he goads patient Theophilus with insults and bullying tactics, even to causing the loss of a hard-won pan of water. Not surprisingly, the boys' teacher considers Theophilus the more deserving of the two, and sets out to help him win the chance for the scholarship. But Theophilus still lacks confidence in his own abilities, and it is not until the teacher plays a "magic" trick on him that he begins to fulfil his potential, get top results to outrank Mark, and win the scholarship.

Even though *The Power* was designed for the international market, it is something of a surprise to find Rhone reverting to standard English for this rural piece, since his vernacular plays have been well received internationally. But whatever language he uses, Pa Trevor, like Pa Ben in *Old Story Time*, tells a good story. Like no other Caribbean playwright, Pa Trevor can make us all "run come", for the pleasure of being made to laugh, made to see, made to think.

Judy Stone
Cheltenham 2008

Judy Stone is the author of Studies in West Indian Literature: Theatre, *and was for many years arts critic and theatre columnist for the* Trinidad Guardian. *She is the editor of the* MCW Gayelle *collections of West Indian plays. For a brief period she worked in partnership with Trevor Rhone, staging dinner theatre at the Hotel Normandie, Port of Spain, after which she ran the continuous theatre programme single-handedly for several years through her independent theatre company, Touchstone Productions.*

Two Can Play

Characters

JIM
GLORIA, his wife

Two Can Play was first staged at the Barn Theatre, Kingston, Jamaica in 1982, directed by Trevor Rhone. The cast was as follows:

> Jim   Charles Hyatt
> Gloria   Grace McGhie

The first television production of *Two Can Play* was produced by PBS TV for Kentucky Educational Television and featured the original stage cast.

The play is set in Kingston, Jamaica, in the late 1970's, in what was once a lower middle income area. The area has been ravaged by the effects of political warfare, and is now a deprived and depressed area, falling just short of being a ghetto.

Two Can Play

The Set   The stage set is the interior of what was formerly a fairly decent looking house, with lattice work, inside bathrooms, etc. The house has become a prison, just as hard to get out of as it is to get into.

There are two main areas:

Area 1: The dining area, with kitchen off it. Part of the kitchen's counter and shelving are visible. There is a window which looks to the outside. The front door entrance to the house is visible. Both window and front door are secured by bolts, pins, and grillwork. In the dining area there is the obligatory shelving which contains the family photographs, crochet doilies and other bric-a-brac.

Area 2: The main bedroom, with a bathroom off it. A window looks to the outside. It is secured by bolts and grillwork.

These two areas are linked by a corridor. One other bedroom door is visible on this corridor.

Central to the setting is the security grill gate, complete with chain, lock and bolts. It separates the sleeping area from the rest of the house.

Act One

Scene 1

[*Incidental reggae music continues over as the house lights go to black. The actors come on in the blackout. The stage lights come up slowly, as gun shots explode in the distance and dogs bark frantically.* JIM *and* GLORIA *are lying in bed.*]

JIM: Gloria?

GLORIA: Yes, Jim
[*Gunshots, dogs barking*]

JIM: Hear dey … is war out dey. [*Gunshots getting louder.*] We under siege tonight, Gloria.

GLORIA: Go to sleep, Jim.

JIM: But Gloria – it getting closer.

GLORIA: Put a pillow over yuh head. [*Barrage of loud gunshots*]

JIM: It gettin' closer still … listen … [GLORIA *gets up off the bed and goes to the bathroom.*] Where yuh going?... Gloria?
[GLORIA *returns with a glass of water. She gives it to him with a pill which she takes from a pillbox kept in the bed head.*]

GLORIA: Here.

JIM: Is what?

GLORIA: The valium.

JIM: A take four already.

GLORIA: Take another one.

JIM: Mi inside like a drug store.

GLORIA: Take it.

[JIM *takes the tablet, pops it into his mouth and washes it down with water.*]

GLORIA: Now, try and sleep.

[*They both lie back in the bed. For a moment there is silence. Then shots, very loud. JIM and GLORIA jump up and look at each other. GLORIA reaches underneath the bed for a bottle of water and a cutlass, and goes towards the grill gate, while* JIM *reaches for a slipper and heads for the clothes closet.*]

JIM: Dat can't do nutten 'gainst M-16 …

GLORIA: Oh yes? Make them come – make them come.

JIM: Gloria, dem shootin' up the house – dem shootin' it up!

GLORIA: Is by the gully.

JIM: No – is right inside here.

[*There is a big blast of automatic gunfire.*]

JIM: We dead! We dead! Gloria, Gloria, we dead!

[*He hides himself in the clothes closet. The gunfire dies down. Slowly he comes out.*]

A could swear it was in the house. It sound like it was right in here. Oh mi God!

GLORIA: Hang on to yuh nerves …

[*She puts her weapons down and then consoles JIM.*]

JIM: A can't take it, Gloria – A can't take it no more …

GLORIA: Pull yuhself together…don't make it get to yuh, Jim or yuh gone to Bellevue …

JIM: Lord have mercy.

GLORIA: One day it muss be over. It can't go on forever.

JIM: Is months now, Gloria; is months.

[GLORIA *hums and then sings a little song: "What a fellowship, what a joy divine, leaning on…" etc.*]

Sister Glo, yuh not 'fraid?

GLORIA: No Jim, 'fraid for what?

    [*Loud blast of gunfire*]

JIM: Hear dey … that one sound like a cannon.

GLORIA: Them call that one 'the Grandfather'.

JIM: Pops! Go check on him.

GLORIA: Him okay.

JIM: Poor ole man. What a way to spend yuh last days. Jesus, it hot. In here is like a furnace. Go for the fan and put it on.

GLORIA: Last month light bill don't pay yet. Open the window.

JIM: Yuh must be mad!

GLORIA: Jim, yuh have to fight fear. Open the window.

JIM: No, Gloria.

GLORIA: Open it, Jim.

    [*Jim walks tentatively toward the window.*]

JIM: Lord, I am opening dis window coz it hot and A can't sleep, so if a bullet come in and blow off mi head, den is thy will and A will see yuh on the odder side. In the event dat A open it and all dat come in is the cool breeze, den yuh will see me right here in the morning. Night, Lord. Night, Glo. Turn off the light.

    [JIM *returns to bed.*]

GLORIA: Jim.

JIM: Is what?

GLORIA: Yuh leave the manure round the front?

JIM: What a time to ask me dat. Yuh really think dey would tief the shit?

GLORIA: It would surprise yuh if yuh wake up in the morning and don't see it?

JIM: No. Turn off the light.

    [GLORIA *flicks off the bedside lamp. They lie in the half light for a while.*]

    Turn back on the light, Gloria.

GLORIA: What now?

JIM: A can't sleep with the window open.

[*He goes across and locks it.*]

What's the time?

GLORIA: One o'clock.

JIM: That's all? Is hours before day break.

GLORIA: Try an' sleep.

JIM: Sleep? Me can't sleep. When A go to work A will sleep. A jus' hate the night time, y'know, Gloria. Five o'clock in the evening is panic time for me, y'know, Gloria.

GLORIA: Try an' relax. Come.

[*He wanders around restlessly.*]

If yuh wasn't so stubborn we would move out of dis neighbourhood long ago.

JIM: No way.

GLORIA: Yuh don't have to play brave with me. A not yuh friends on the corner. A hear yuh wid dem all the time, "Dem have to kill me – dem not making me move."

JIM: Gloria, we can't afford uptown house.

GLORIA: Say dat …

JIM: I born in dis neighbourhood – mi friends in dis neighbourhood. I am all right – me nuh 'fraid.

[*Shots*]

Lord … Give me another valium. Mi mind dashing all over the place … the situation here – Pops – the children …

GLORIA: If yuh was to hear that the children okay, yuh would feel better?

JIM: Boy, Gloria! A would give mi eyeball to hear dat.

GLORIA: A hear from Andrew. Him write.

JIM: Jesus Christ! What yuh saying to me! Him write? Yuh crazy woman? Gloria, what A tell dem when dem was leaving? Gloria … what A tell dem? If A sick, don't write. If dem hear A dead, don't communicate. Don't phone. Yuh know why A tell dem dat?

7

GLORIA: Yes, Jim.

JIM: So why the ass yuh encourage dem to disobey mi orders?

GLORIA: A never encourage them, Jim.

JIM: Yuh never discourage dem either. Yuh notice them don't write to me. After all the trouble and the sacrifice to get them there. Yuh know them can trace that letter ...

GLORIA: Trace what!

JIM: Uncle Sam is a bitch. Him have satellite up in the sky can read the number on dis house. Any return address on the letter?

GLORIA: No, Jim.

JIM: At least him have that much sense. Him sign him name?

GLORIA: Just 'Boogsie'.

JIM: Oh ...

GLORIA: Jesus Christ, man! Why yuh so paranoid?

JIM: Paranoid? A not paranoid; mi nerves on edge, that's all. Gloria, them is illegal immigrant. Them convert the one entry, one week visa to permanent. One mistake, one slip-up, and they right back here. A tell them, go underground, get lost, don't give Uncle Sam a chance to catch you. What Andrew say? Him not in any trouble?

GLORIA: Him OK.

JIM: Lord be praised!

GLORIA: And him see Paul ...

JIM: Him really see Paul?

GLORIA: They meet on the subway.

JIM: Mi boys riding subway. Them gone underground in truth. A can imagine how they feel when they meet each other.

GLORIA: They living together.

JIM: Bad move dat. If they catch one, they catch two ...

GLORIA: Paul have three job.

JIM: Three jobs. Lord have mercy. Three jobs. One for every year him never work out here.

[*He goes down on his knees.*]

God bless America – God bless America.

GLORIA: And Andrew going to school full time …

JIM: God bless America.

GLORIA: Paul supporting him.

JIM: Paul mi boy, like father like son. Yuh don't resemble me for nutten. Sending yuh little brother to school. Ai mi children. A was right to send dem away. Gloria, don't A was right?

[*Long pause*]

I love them too, Gloria. We tried with them here. You know how we sacrificed to send Paul to high school. For what? To sit on the corner for three years and keep bad company. Is prayers why the police never shoot him down …

[*Pause – silence.*]

GLORIA: Andrew say he miss home.

[*Sound of gun shots*]

JIM: Listen to that. Is that him miss?

GLORIA: Is America the guns come from.

JIM: Or Cuba. A don't know. All A know is, we talking about survival. What about Suzie? Any word?

[*Pause*]

GLORIA: No …

[*She cries.*]

JIM: Look don't start. A want to cry too. So don't cry. Trust in the Lord. Uncle Sam will see them go right.

GLORIA: They don't belong to Uncle Sam.

JIM: Suzie sensible. A talk to her before A put her on the plane.

GLORIA: Jim, where she sleep that first night? She sixteen and we just abandon her so …

JIM: A never abandon her.

GLORIA: Is what den? A still can't believe I allow yuh to send her away …

9

JIM: Is because yuh don't know what was happening to her out here. Is the whorehouse A rescue her from one day.

GLORIA: Suzie?!!

JIM: Two bad gal down the road inveigle her. Pops get word of it, and A bring her home. She promise to look something better. And if she go to America and whore, is better if we don't see. Yuh don't feel so too?

GLORIA: My Suzie?

JIM: Face facts, Gloria. She never had a chance in this environment.

GLORIA: Is not the environment fail her.

JIM: I give them more than I ever get. Them at least get some schooling. A did mi best, and when man on earth has done his best, angels can do no better. I don't fail them. Paul have three job and Andrew going to school. All they would have if they was still here would be me, you, and frustration. We couldn't help them any more. A know it hard but is life. First thing in the morning A will tell Pops the good news. Him going be so happy; the way him love him grandchildren. Andrew ask for him?

GLORIA: Yes.

JIM: A know, man. Is him favourite from time.

GLORIA: The house so lonely and quiet without dem …

JIM: Paul have three jobs and Andrew going to school …

[*Beat – coughing. Pause.*]

GLORIA: Is Pops coughing so?

[*JIM listens briefly. Then he dashes toward the old man's room. He quickly returns.*]

JIM: Get out the tablets.

[*JIM searches for and finds the key that opens the grill door. He opens it and exits towards the kitchen, as GLORIA continues to search for the pills. Sound of water bottle as it drops and breaks. Jim returns from kitchen with the water.*]

10

Careful if yuh go in the kitchen. Pop's water bottle drop from me and buss. Pass the tablets.

GLORIA: A can't find them.

JIM: How yuh mean?

GLORIA: Dem not in here.

JIM: Yuh check the bathroom?

GLORIA: Yes, but is here A keep them.

JIM: But is only last week A fill the prescription.

GLORIA: Is last week's date on dis.

[*He takes the pill bottle and examines it.*]

JIM: They couldn't finish already. A don't understand.

[*Laboured coughing, increasing in intensity*]

Go stay with him. I will call a doctor.

GLORIA: Which doctor yuh getting to come here at dis hour? Dem don't even come in the day.

[JIM *picks up the directory, looking for a number.*]

JIM: Maybe him can treat him over the phone.

[JIM *dials.*]

GLORIA: Is the tablets him need.

JIM: Then look for them. Jesus Christ! Answer the phone man... Hello – Doctor? Emergency! Mi father **on** dying... Rollington Town area... Yes, I can understand that, but the man is dying. Him swell up, hand, foot, everything... Yes, him have a history of high blood pressure... Ah, 72 next month... yes... yes, Doctor... DIGO, X,I,N. Somehow it finish.

[*Intense coughing and gasping*]

GLORIA: Him coughing blood, Jim.

JIM: Him coughing blood now, Doctor...

GLORIA: And froth, plenty, white looking stuff.

JIM: And froth, plenty, white looking stuff... What is your address, Doctor?

[JIM *grabs a pencil by the phone – he writes.*]

Eleven Tulip Drive, Norbrook...

[JIM *hangs up the phone and turns to* GLORIA.]

GLORIA: What him say?

JIM: Him have some of the tablets at him house. If we want we can come for them.

GLORIA: Is 1:30 in the morning, taxi not coming down here.

JIM: Yuh think him can hold out till daylight?

GLORIA: Bwoy Jim. A don't think... and anyway, we can't take dat chance...

JIM: Rass!!

[POPS *coughs – gunshots – they look at each other.*]

GLORIA: Yuh might go out and...Oh Jesus, what a life! You have to try and get them Jim, somehow.

JIM: But Gloria...

GLORIA: If you can get out by the main, chances are yuh might pick up a taxi.

JIM: Yes. Yes.

[*Starts to dress*]

You got today, yesterday *Star*?

GLORIA: Here.

JIM: As A thought.

GLORIA: What?

JIM: Curfew.

GLORIA: No matter. Yuh have to try and get through. Is a matter of life or death.

JIM: But is war outside, Gloria.

GLORIA: No Jim, dat is madness. Even in war the wounded get a chance to get treatment.

[JIM *opens a window and looks out.*]

JIM: Rass!

GLORIA: What's the doctor's address?

[*She takes some clothes from the closet and she too starts to dress.*]

JIM: What yuh doing? Where yuh going?

GLORIA: One of us have to go Jim.

JIM: But Gloria, yuh might go out an' man rape yuh, gun yuh down.

GLORIA: A have to take dat chance.

JIM: The valium have me groggy…

GLORIA: Is O.K. Yuh stay and look after him. Hot some water and clean him up.

JIM: Light the stove for me nuh.

[GLORIA *looks at him with a mixture of disgust and bitterness, annoyed at his ineffectualness. She then exits toward the kitchen, cursing him under her breath. Sound of* GLORIA *falling. She speaks from offstage.*]

GLORIA: Jesus! Oh Lawd! Aieeee…

JIM: Gloria! What happen?

[*He crosses to the kitchen.*]

GLORIA: Is yuh buss the water bottle in here?

JIM: A did tell yuh…

GLORIA: Why yuh never clean it up?

JIM: A was rushing. Yuh O.K.?

GLORIA: A think A buss mi hip…

JIM: Come, let me help yuh inside.

[*As he helps her to the dining area, coughing is heard offstage.*]

GLORIA: Me okay. Pops!!

[*He leaves her and goes toward the bedroom to finish dressing, as she shuffles to the door and starts pulling the bolts. On the third bolt, the church bell tolls. As the lights dim, they both freeze momentarily. Then* GLORIA *sings a sad mournful song as* JIM *dresses for the funeral. He exits through* POPS' *room.* GLORIA *changes the tablecloth to a white one. Then she leaves for the bedroom. Still singing, she drapes the mirror with a black cloth, also ties her head with black material.*]

13

Having done so she returns to the dining table to sit on the down right chair. The tolling continues over till she sits and rests her head on the table, eyes closed.]

Act One, Scene 2

[*The lights go up to full on* GLORIA, *her head resting on the table, her eyes closed. It is evening, about 8:00, five days later.* JIM *enters through the front door. He is dressed in a muddied black suit, with his tie slightly askew.*]

JIM: Sister Glo, Sister Glo…
    [*She speaks as she wakes.*]
GLORIA: Yuh come?
JIM: Hm, how yuh feeling?
GLORIA: Nuh bad. How it went?
JIM: Aye Glo…
GLORIA: What happen?
JIM: Is what never happen. Let me change dem clothes…
    [*He moves toward the bedroom.*]
GLORIA: Lawd God, how yuh dirty up so Jim?
JIM: Is a long story Glo.
    [*He tries to walk away.*]
    Oooh…
    [*He holds his back.*]
GLORIA: What happen to yuh back? Yuh hurt yuhself?
JIM: Put it dis way – we both is invalids tonight; none to help the other. Oh, Lawd!
    [GLORIA *struggles across to help him take off his jacket.*]
GLORIA: What happen?
    [*She removes the jacket.*]

14

JIM: Glo, I give mi heart to dis country. A love the place. I am a good citizen; I pay mi taxes, A don't have any choice. A pay mi Housing Trust, although A don't have any benefit to get. I give mi sweat, mi tears, mi love. A had to send away mi children. What more dey want? Mi blood?

GLORIA: What happen Jim?

JIM: Wherever him is now, him happy. Him is out of dis misery. Walk good, Pops, walk good. Take care o' yuhself.
[*He cries.*]

GLORIA: Is all right, is all right.
[*She reaches out to him.*]
How yuh hurt yuhself?

JIM: Them let go the coffin on me…

GLORIA: How yuh mean?

JIM: When the shoot-out start.

GLORIA: Shoot-out? What shoot-out?

JIM: One shoot-out by the graveside today! One shoot-out! A pick the wrong day to bury the old man. Remember the whole heap o' gunfire the night Pops take in sick?

GLORIA: Yes…

JIM: It was political warfare. One high-ranking capitalist gunman dead the night…

GLORIA: And is today them decide to bury him…

JIM: With full honours. Twenty-one gun salute…right side where Pops suppose to bury.

GLORIA: Lord ha' mercy!

JIM: In the middle of the twenty-one gun salute, the socialist faction arrive…

GLORIA: I can see it; don't tell me any more!

JIM: Them say the dead not buryin', coz the cemetery is in dem territory. And is den the gun battle really start. On the first volley, the pall-bearers who carrying Pops drop the coffin and take foot for it. Them let it go on me. The whole of mi

15

back wrench out one time…oh Jesus!

[*He feels a stab of pain.*]

GLORIA: Yuh better let me rub something on it…

[*JIM waves her off.*]

JIM: The parson, give him him due, never run yet, but when a shot take away him wife handbag, A hear him say, "Let the dead bury the dead, come woman!"

GLORIA: Oh mi God! Poor Pops.

JIM: The timid wife him have there, like she can't mash ants, well she bulldoze three gravestones in her getaway. All dis time A still hang on to Pops. A hang on for dear life. A wasn't running. It was death before humiliation. A hang on till A feel something whistle past mi ears, and A say to miself, "Pops gone already, no further harm can come to him," so A put him down. A couldn't run, even if A did want to. So A lie down beside him and is him save mi life…

GLORIA: Just like Pops…

JIM: It wasn't until the police arrive dat things quieten down. A was about six feet from the grave and somehow A manage to get the coffin over to it. When A look in the grave, who yuh think A see down there? Nuh the parson man. One piece o' prayers… "Oh Lord as yuh raised Lazarus from the dead, deliver me from dis grave." A help to pull him out.

GLORIA: And him help yuh bury him?

JIM: Man never even tell me thanks. The parson run, Gloria. Him dat teach me bout faith and prayer, and how to face adversity, him run.

GLORIA: So what about the last rites?

JIM: A bury the old man miself, Glo. I say the prayers and I sing the hymn, "Will the circle be unbroken by and by Lord, There's a better home awaits me in the sky Lord, in the sky."

[GLORIA *cries.*]

A bury him, Glo, and as A walk out of the cemetery I make a decision. The effing gunman and the effing politician not controlling my existence ever again. I taking control of mi life from today. If that could happen to Pops… A remember the night him took in sick, A took mi life in mi hand and head out into the street. Is nuh little run A run dat night yuh know Gloria… A run…

GLORIA: A pray…

JIM: A dodge…

GLORIA: Is in my arms him dead. Oh my God, I don't want to remember it.

JIM: A took mi life into mi hands and head out into the street.

GLORIA: A thought you would never make it back.

JIM: Is nuh little run A run dat night, you know, Gloria. A run…

GLORIA: Him squeeze mi hand and him hold me tight, and him say, "Daughter…"

JIM: A run…

GLORIA: A pray…

JIM: A run, A run, A run. And still A couldn't get through. Them kill Pops! Dis effing country kill Pops. Gloria, believe yuh me when A tell yuh, I want no more part of dis country, and the fuss chance A get to get out, I gone!

GLORIA: Yuh must be hungry.

JIM: A don't want any food, A just want to get out.

GLORIA: Eat first.

JIM: I am full up to here.

[JIM *indicates his neck.*]

GLORIA: Let me get something for miself then…

JIM: All right… bring me a little something.

[GLORIA *goes into the kitchen.*]

Gloria, the children don't know.

GLORIA: They will know somehow.

17

JIM: Somehow how?

GLORIA: A will... trust in the Lord. Him will get word to them.

JIM: Is just as well them not here. After that experience A go through today...

[*Pause...* GLORIA *speaks as she comes out of the kitchen.*]

GLORIA: It on the fire.

[*There is a pause.*]

JIM: The house quiet, enh?

GLORIA: Not even a gunshot tonight. A can't remember the place so quiet; if it wasn't the children, it was Pops.

JIM: A go miss him yuh know, Gloria...

GLORIA: Me too.

JIM: A serious, yuh know...

GLORIA: About what?

JIM: Migrate.

GLORIA: Is not so much that A wanted to go Jim. Is just that A didn't want the children up there by themselves.

JIM: Why Pops die? Yuh know? Them tablets never finish just so, y'know. Pops realize that if yuh ever get the chance, yuh would go find the children.

GLORIA: But Jim, him...

JIM: Is so. Pops clear the way. Is him throw away the tablets.

GLORIA: Don't make me feel like is me kill him...

JIM: No, Glo. I know yuh did love him, but Pops did what him thought was best.

GLORIA: But dat is suicide, Jim!

JIM: No Glo, sacrifice. We have to go. Pops say so. We can't let him down. So Uncle Sam, we don't know how we coming yet but watch out, coz we coming!

[BLACKOUT]

18

Act One, Scene 3

[*It is late afternoon. JIM is by the refrigerator with a plate in his hands. A small piece of chicken sits in it. He licks his fingers, then returns the plate to the refrigerator. He is heading toward the bedroom when he stops and retraces his steps to the fridge, opens it, takes out the plate, devours the last piece of chicken, and then replaces the plate. He slams the fridge shut and is again heading toward the bedroom when he stops, returns to the fridge, drinks water from the bottle, wipes his hands on a dish cloth which is tied to the refrigerator door, and heads towards the bedroom. At this time, GLORIA, dressed in a duster, is coming in from the bathroom. She is carrying a brown paper bag with a carton of cigarettes in it. The paper bag is tightly wrapped to conceal the cigarettes.*]

JIM: Yuh bring a *Star*?

GLORIA: No. A never see any. Here.

[*She hands JIM a blank passport application form.*]

JIM: Is what?

GLORIA: The passport application form.

[*JIM takes it from her.*]

GLORIA: Yuh take yuh passport picture yet?

JIM: Tomorrow. But we still don't know how we getting up there and A not going up there underground, so we stuck…

GLORIA: Tell Pops that. What yuh think him would say?

JIM: Yuh right. We have to find a way…

GLORIA: Whatever the obstacle, Jim. And right now we have to save as much money as we can.

JIM: We can sell the house…

GLORIA: And if we ever decide to come back?

JIM: Once me step, Gloria, me step.

GLORIA: Even if we was to rent it…

JIM: Yuh would collect the first month rent and that's it. Sell!

19

GLORIA: Nobody buying.

JIM: We can't lock it up… them would capture it before we reach airport.

GLORIA: So what we going do, walk away and leave it? After how we sacrifice to get it? Is not the house so much as the fruit trees. Go water the orange tree for me. Put the hose at the root. It might yet blossom before we have to leave it. A will go look after yuh supper.

[GLORIA *pushes him out. She takes up the package and looks through the window to make sure that he is outside. She then takes a carton of cigarettes from the package and hides it under the dining table. She then goes to the refrigerator. She sees the empty plate.*]

GLORIA: Wretch!

[*She puts the plate in the sink, then returns to the bedroom, collects her make-up kit, returns to the dining room table, and proceeds to do her nails – all the while she is singing a hymn to keep her spirits up.* JIM *is re-entering.*]

JIM: Gloria, yuh don't start cook yet?

[*She sings louder.*]

Gloria, I am talking to yuh.

GLORIA: No, Jim, A don't start cook yet.

JIM: I hungry bad. What yuh have to eat?

[*He heads into the kitchen.*]

GLORIA: Nutten in there.

[JIM *retraces his steps and heads to the refrigerator.*]

Nutten in there, either.

JIM: Nutten? Not even to make a sandwich?

GLORIA: Nutten.

JIM: Stop paint up yuhself and go cook nuh Gloria…

GLORIA: Mi nails stay bad enh?

JIM: Gloria, what is dis thing yuh take up of late?

GLORIA: I can't do somet'ing for miself?

20

JIM: So what happen to me? Leave dat! Go cook!

GLORIA: Not dis evening, Jim. Drink some water and go to yuh bed.

JIM: Gloria, yuh chatting nonsense.

GLORIA: What happen to the leftovers in the fridge?

JIM: Leftovers?

GLORIA: Yes, the chicken wing.

JIM: A was feeling a little peckish and…

GLORIA: Dat was yuh supper.

JIM: Gloria, A tired sacrifice!

[*He goes into the bedroom, takes out a shirt, and prepares to go out.*]

GLORIA: Dat chicken was to share for me and yuh.

JIM: Dat little morsel a…

GLORIA: Yes, and I am without supper coz a you and yuh damn selfishness. One person alone can't be expected to sacrifice. Yuh sure that yuh serious about this going to America?

JIM: How yuh mean!

GLORIA: Well then, get serious. So far A don't see any effort from yuh. All A hear is "Lard Gloria, A hungry." No more food buying till tomorrow. One night without food won't kill yuh, but it should teach yuh a lesson. Eat off everything one day, yuh do without the next. Yuh have to tighten yuh belt.

[JIM *returns to the dining room. He is almost fully dressed.*]

JIM: The money yuh spen' buying war paint, could buy extra food.

GLORIA: Jim, A have not spent a penny on miself in twenty years.

JIM: And is now yuh starting. Yuh tell me about sacrifice and tighten mi belt. Is sacrifice dis?

[*He picks up her nail polish.*]

GLORIA: Yuh still have money for yuh cigarette though?

21

JIM: Have which money? For what cigarette?

[GLORIA *takes out a cigarette box.*]

Cigarettes! Where yuh get cigarettes?

GLORIA: No bother long out yuh tongue.

[JIM *reaches for it.*]

Hands off!

JIM: Come nuh, Sister Glo. Free me. From morning A don't smoke a cigarette…

GLORIA: So, why yuh never buy?

JIM: A don't have nuh money. And not one in the shop. They like gold out a street. Where yuh get dat?

GLORIA: Contacts.

JIM: Come nuh…

GLORIA: Where me and yuh going?

JIM: Don't be unreasonable Gloria. A can do without food, but ease me up with a smoke…

GLORIA: I buy them to sell.

JIM: Sell me one, then.

GLORIA: A thought yuh never had any money?

JIM: Yuh nuh will credit me.

[GLORIA *laughs.*]

GLORIA: Today A saw a man pay ten cents for a puff. How much puff in a cigarette?

JIM: About ten to fifteen.

GLORIA: One dollar fifty.

[*She is holding out her hand.*]

JIM: Shit! For what?

GLORIA: Seeing as is you, give me a dollar.

JIM: Yuh mad…

GLORIA: Take it or leave it. Is forty dollar A pay for the carton.

JIM: Is a carton yuh have!

[*He goes in search of the carton.*]

22

GLORIA: And don't bother look for them. A want to make at least sixty dollar profit. A won't satisfy with less.

[GLORIA *rests an empty cigarette box on the table.*]

JIM: Yuh is a damn little capitalist.

GLORIA: A praying for the strike prolong, push up the price.

[JIM *is re-entering, sees the pack and inches towards it – he grabs it, triumphant. He opens it. It is empty.*]

JIM: Don't do me them things.

[GLORIA *produces a single cigarette.*]

A will pay yuh later.

GLORIA: No Jim. A know yuh. Put the money on the table.

JIM: A only have eighty cents.

GLORIA: Bring the razor blade…

[JIM *goes to find a razor blade, then stops.*]

JIM: Yuh going cut it? See the twenty cents…

GLORIA: On the table.

[JIM *complies.* GLORIA *gives him the cigarette, then packs up nail polish, etc., and goes into the bedroom.* JIM *seizes the cigarette with real pleasure and looks around for matches.*]

JIM: Yuh see the matches?

GLORIA: Matches short.

[JIM *continues to look away from* GLORIA, *who rattles a box. He looks around.*]

JIM: Gimme a light.

GLORIA: Ten cents a stick. Put it on the bed.

JIM: Sister Gloria…

GLORIA: Don't "Sister Gloria" me. As a matter of fact, get matches where yuh going.

JIM: Where yuh see me going?

GLORIA: G'wan…

JIM: A just going down the road…

GLORIA: Yuh going to EAT something.

JIM: How yuh could say a thing like that?

GLORIA: What A say? Notice A don't ask yuh to bring a *piece* for me, coz it wouldn't be to my liking. Today is Tuesday, not even the gunman can keep yuh away from dat little sweetheart.

JIM: Gloria, yuh chatting nonsense. What little sweetheart? A will lock the gate. A soon come...

GLORIA: Jim, the children not here. Pops gone. Yuh have no reason to lock me in any more.

JIM: What yuh mean by that?

GLORIA: Take care of yuhself.

JIM: Yuh too...

GLORIA: I will do just that.

[*She storms into the bedroom, going directly into the bathroom and slamming the door.*]

JIM: Is what do her sah?

[BLACKOUT]

Act One, Scene 4

[JIM *comes on from* POPS's *room. He unlocks the grill gate and continues into the dining area. He gets an idea. He goes to the phone and dials, speaks on phone.*]

JIM: Hey, what's happening? Yuh have anything to eat?... Eh?... At home. She gone supermarket... Hey, listen now, las' night was the greatest y'know... Honest. The greatest. Is like you make a special effort... True... True... The greatest A telling you. Is the greatest plate o' stew peas me ever taste in mi life.

[GLORIA *is heard calling from off.*]

GLORIA: Jim!

    [JIM *starts and hurriedly whispers into the phone.*]

JIM: A gone. See you Tuesday.

    [*He hangs up.*]

GLORIA: Jim!

JIM: Oi.

GLORIA: Open the door for me…

JIM: Coming…

    [*He unlocks the bolts and* GLORIA *comes on with two parcels of groceries.*]

    Why yuh come home so late?

    [*He takes a parcel from her.*]

GLORIA: Is three supermarket A had to go to. One riot to get a little rice.

JIM: Yuh get bread?

    [*He bolts the door.*]

GLORIA: Not even a slice.

JIM: Yuh get flour, though?

GLORIA: Get what.

JIM: Serious thing y'know. Is famine on the land.

GLORIA: Yuh can eat out what A get y'see. Is for the week. Jus' rest it on the table.

    [*She leaves the dining area with toilet articles, which she takes into the bedroom. At the same time* JIM *explores the shopping bag, coming up with a roll of toilet paper, then another, then a tin of cleanser – as* GLORIA *is returning.*]

JIM: Gloria.

GLORIA: Enh?

    [JIM *notices what she is wearing.*]

JIM: Is mad yuh mad, or is stupid, yuh stupid, or what?

GLORIA: What A do now?

JIM: Is so yuh go to work?

GLORIA: What wrong with me?

25

JIM: Orange and green. Yuh is a walking target for either side.

GLORIA: A like the combination.

[*She starts to unpack the groceries.*]

JIM: Vanity will be the death of yuh, woman. From now on is brown or blue. Yuh have to dress neutral.

GLORIA: A tired of the madness.

JIM: A school pickney almost meet her death the other day, coz of the colour of her uniform. Nobody didn't say anything to yuh on the road?

GLORIA: People was looking on me, yes...

JIM: So, what yuh think? Is admire dem was admiring yuh?

GLORIA: Come. A want to talk to yuh.

[*She heads toward the bedroom and closes the windows.*]

JIM: Is what?... Don't lock up the house yet...

GLORIA: Shh... Shh. A don't want nobody know mi business. Read that.

[*She gives him a folded newspaper. He reads from it.*]

JIM: "Want to get to America..."

[*They look at each other.*]

GLORIA: A went to see him today.

[*She hands JIM a card.*]

Him staying at the Terra Nova.

JIM: Charles E. Wright – Immigration Consultant... Suite 123, Miami. What colour is dis man?

GLORIA: Black, Jamaican, originally from Catadupa, St James. Him was talking about ackee and saltfish, blue-drawers an' all dem thing...

JIM: Could be a trap to get yuh confidence. He could be a C. I.A. agent. Uncle Sam smart. Trust nobody.

GLORIA: We might as well forget it then Jim, coz we can't get up there by weself.

[*She moves away.*]

JIM: Gloria! Gloria, Gloria… A tell yuh what – A will check him out. Yuh never mention the children?

GLORIA: No.

JIM: Good. What him had to say?

GLORIA: Him suggest a thing name "Identikit".

JIM: What dat?

GLORIA: Him will supply us with a completely new identify. Yuh get it?

JIM: No.

GLORIA: Jim… Identikit…

[*He looks blank.*]

We give him we age, an two photograph. Him have a contact in Alabama who will go to a cemetery…

JIM: Cemetery! Don't mention dat word to me!

GLORIA: Him go to the cemetery an' check for a man who born the same year as you. Den him go to the Records Office of Births and Deaths, where him contact have a contact who will destroy the man Death Certificate…

JIM: Hold on, yuh going too fast…

GLORIA: Him use your picture, an' the dead man birth certificate to apply for a passport…

JIM: In the dead man name?

GLORIA: It can't be in your name, Jim. Him will do the same for me. Let's say the man name…

JIM: Mr Lazarus…

GLORIA: Yuh t'ink yuh funny, yuh know…

JIM: If the man come back from the dead, what yuh expect him to name?

GLORIA: Yuh will get a complete record of him life… from the day him born…

JIM: Till the day him dead…

GLORIA: Jim, the man nuh dead…

27

JIM: A get it now! As far as the world is concerned, the man is still alive…

GLORIA: Yes, Jim, an' yuh going to take him place. Yuh passport will show dat yuh arrive in Jamaica for a holiday, so when yuh arrive back in the U.S., yuh just join the returning residents line, and in two twos, yuh gone clear.

JIM: Stop!

GLORIA: What?

JIM: A don't like it.

GLORIA: What wrong with it?

JIM: Let me show yuh what wrong with it. Let's imagine dis is Miami airport. You is Lady Lazarus and yuh arrive from Jamaica, and I is the Immigration Officer standing behind mi desk.

[On these words, JIM moves to stand behind the bed head, using it as a desk.]

GLORIA: Yuh never travel, yet, so what yuh coming with?

JIM: I fix phone at airport. I know how it go… Come!

[JIM hands her a novel to use as a passport. He sucks at his teeth, begins to chew imaginary gum. He then looks her up and down, and speaks in a pseudo-American accent.]

Git behind the red line, lady.

[GLORIA plays the game. JIM keeps his eyes on the desk in impersonal fashion and stretches out a hand.]

Passport, Madame!

[GLORIA hands it to him. He takes it and, continuing with the imaginary gum chewing, thumbs through it, while looking her up and down. GLORIA has returned to the imaginary red line. JIM continues to look at her suspiciously for a little while. She becomes a little uncomfortable.]

GLORIA: Excuse me. A have to go the bathroom.

[She is exiting when JIM stops her.]

JIM: Yuh wretch! Yuh peepee up yuhself right there. A was just waiting to hear yuh accent. As yuh open yuh mouth, the man would buss out a laugh an' call the police. A don't like "Identikit". Him don't suggest anything else?

GLORIA: Yeah, but it kinda roundabout.

JIM: It muss be better dan dis Lazarus thing. Let me hear it nuh...

GLORIA: Yuh would have to divorce me.

JIM: No suh! Me not into that. Forget it! After the divorce, what happen?

GLORIA: What a way yuh change yuh mind fast.

JIM: A curious, dat's all.

GLORIA: Den yuh would marry a US citizen. Few months pass, dat divorce come through, yuh legal. A come up, we married again, two o' we legal...

JIM: Then suppose the woman like me?

GLORIA: A know yuh would think o'dat.

JIM: You read me wrong dis time. An' even if it was so, A would resist her. What A meant was, what if she like me an' want to hold on to me against mi will?

GLORIA: Before yuh married, she would have to sign a paper agreeing to a divorce.

JIM: Ah see what yuh mean. It could work, yes. What yuh say?

GLORIA: No. A know yuh. Bout if she like yuh. How yuh going to resist? Is the last A would see of yuh.

JIM: Gloria, how yuh chat so much nonsense. Look how long you and me married. Seriously what yuh think?

GLORIA: A have to think 'bout it. Marriage is a sacred thing.

JIM: Yuh rather go to Miami, go peepee up yuhself...

GLORIA: An' if the children was to hear...

JIM: How them to hear. This is a good plan. No risks involved.

GLORIA: On what grounds?

JIM: Time is of the essence. What is the fastest?

GLORIA: Adultery.

JIM: Who commit it?

GLORIA: You!

JIM: Me?!

GLORIA: Up to last Tuesday.

[JIM *laughs*.]

JIM: Gloria…

GLORIA: What yuh laughing for?

JIM: Yuh make funny joke. A must laugh.

GLORIA: Joke nuh! Yuh think A don't know?

JIM: Gloria, yuh chatting nonsense. A get it! We tell two lie. Say yuh desert the matrimonial home ten years ago. A get two friends swear to it; few weeks later we single again. What yuh say?

GLORIA: It going set we back $2,500 US - Delivered…

JIM: Blouse beat!

GLORIA: We have to raise it, Jim.

JIM: See the Immigration Consultant. Tell him the deal is on. We will contact him when we ready.

GLORIA: Him leaving Thursday. We will have to contact him in Miami…

JIM: On the phone? No sah! Letter worse…

GLORIA: Maybe we could organize a code…

JIM: Ahm, yes, something like, we got the "H'onions"…

GLORIA: Nuh bad!

JIM: Touch me…

[*They laugh.*]

Gloria…

GLORIA: Mmmm…

JIM: What we would do if dis man was to carry down we life savings?

GLORIA: Hmm, boy Jim, A would have to leave him to God, coz me wouldn't have the heart to pay the $5.00 to kill him.

JIM: If we have $5.00. Hmm… anyhow… where we getting the
     US money?

GLORIA: It on the street.

JIM: Right side the counterfeit?

GLORIA: Is okay. I can get a machine to test the money.

JIM: What kind o' machine?

GLORIA: A little thing, bout dis size. Yuh pass the money over
     it, and if a red light come on it good.

JIM: Get it. Passing them F.I.U. boys at the airport going call for
     some real strategy. Gloria, yuh go cook while A put some
     brain power to dis. Now…
     [GLORIA *gets up and is heading to the kitchen.*]
     Now where on yuh can A hide dat money?
     [GLORIA *stops in surprise.*]

GLORIA: On me? Stop a minute. Is me going up there? A
     thought it was you, Jim.

JIM: A will go yes, but seeing as how yuh have yuh passport
     already…

GLORIA: Ah yuh don't even take your picture yet…

JIM: Gloria…

GLORIA: A tell yuh what, Jim, seeing as how A have to do
     everything. Tomorrow A will go and take yuh picture for yuh.
     [*She leaves the bedroom and goes to the kitchen.*]

JIM: Dat would be a great help. What yuh say? Yuh think yuh
     funny, y'know.
     [*He follows to the bedroom door.* GLORIA *begins to lay the
     table. She
     emphasizes her words by plonking down the table mats,
     plates, knives,
     forks, etc.*]

GLORIA: More than that… let me hold mi tongue. No problem,
     seeing as how A know that when is time to go on the plane,
     is me going have to go. But dere will be a day of reckoning.

31

The sheep to one side, and the goats to the other.

[*She goes towards the bedroom.*]

Let me tell yuh something. A not carrying it in either of those two places...

[JIM *goes off into bathroom and returns with squeezed out toothpaste tube. He tries to get a $2.00 bill into the mouth of the tube. It goes in a little way.*]

JIM: How them say it work? It nuh work. Gimme time. A must come up with something original to beat them F.I.U. boys.

[JIM *looks around. He sees a Kodak instamatic camera. He looks through it as if to take a picture. He then opens it, takes out the cartridge, and throws the cartridge on the bed.*]

Hmm, hmm...

[*He rolls the money, and stuffs it into the camera.*]

This is it! Sister Glo! A get it! A get it! Come quick! This is it!

GLORIA: What happen, why yuh making so much noise?

[*She comes into the bedroom to see* JIM *with camera in hand, twirling it away.*]

JIM: Ha, check dat.

GLORIA: But, Jim. A can see the money showing through...

JIM: Is so? All yuh have to do is cover it over with yuh hand.

GLORIA: Try again. Is not a bad idea.

[*She goes off into the bathroom.* JIM *rests the camera on the bed head and then picks up the toothpaste tube, trying to open the hole as* GLORIA *shouts from bathroom.*]

How come the toothpaste squeeze out all over the bathroom?

[*She comes out into the bedroom.*]

JIM: I was trying to figure out a way to get the money into the tube.

GLORIA: Then that nuh easy, Jim...

JIM: Do it then, if it is so easy.

GLORIA: First thing, yuh shouldn't squeeze out the toothpaste, that not necessary. All yuh have to do is open the bottom, wrap the money in a piece o'plastic, and push it up, and seal it back. Easy as cheese.

JIM: A never realize the bottom could open. How yuh figure it out?

GLORIA: Common sense.

JIM: Yuh see somebody do it. You couldn't figure it out by yuhself.

GLORIA: Why yuh always think A is a damn ass? A figure it out months ago.

JIM: How come, an' is jus' dis' evening we start work on it?

GLORIA: How yuh think the children carry money to America? A wasn't sending them on the plane with $56.00 US.

JIM: An' yuh never say a word to me.

GLORIA: A couldn't say anything to yuh. Yuh too nervous, an' them never stop one o' the children.

JIM: A don't trus' you, y'know.

[*He continues to fiddle with the toothpaste tube while* GLORIA *absentmindedly picks up the camera.*]

GLORIA: Make it rest. Same way the Lord help the children of Israel out of the land of Egypt, him will help us.

[*As she talks she fiddles with the camera.*]

If somehow…

JIM: What, Glo?

GLORIA: Where the cartridge?

[JIM *points to it on the bed.* GLORIA *picks it up.*]

Lend me two dollar.

[JIM *gives it to her.*]

Imagine dis is a US hundred dollar bill. Lord…

[*As she says a silent prayer, then tries to put the money into the cartridge.*]

GLORIA: It going in, Jim! It going in!
JIM: It going in, Glo!
GLORIA: It gone in, Jim.
[JIM *takes the cartridge and camera from her and puts cartridge in camera.*]
JIM: What A tell yuh 'bout me, man.
[*Then he sings.*]
Onward Christian Soldiers…
[*He puts the camera to his eyes, focusing on GLORIA as he continues singing.*]
Click!!

[BLACKOUT]

Act One, Scene 5

[*"Onward Christian Soldiers" continues until the lights come up again. GLORIA enters from the bathroom, goes to the dining area, and looks through the peepholes at the side of the front door. There is no one there – she fidgets, checks the time, takes water from the refrigerator but does not drink. She returns to the window, looks again and sees JIM . She unbolts the front door. JIM comes on immediately.*]

GLORIA: Yuh get it?
JIM: Yes.
GLORIA: Yuh tes' it?
JIM: No. Not yet.
GLORIA: Jesus Christ, Jim!
JIM: It wasn't convenient.
GLORIA: How yuh mean?

34

JIM: Is a dread place A had to go to. A couldn't tes' it in front of the men.

GLORIA: Why not? Is money we dealing with.

JIM: The men touchy y'know. Them don't know me. Yuh don't understand. Is a contact of a contract. Next thing A bring out the tester to test the money, they think A is undercover police and shoot me. To tell you the truth. A never thought A would leave there alive. Suppose me contact set me up – A had an uneasy feeling that somebody was following me. One round d' round A had to take to come home.

GLORIA: Yuh really go buy puss in a bag Jim. Dey would have to kill me. What now if is counterfeit yuh get?

JIM: Don't say so... test it and make me know mi fate.

GLORIA: Is me must test it? No Sir! If we get carry down, we get carry down already.

JIM: Don't talk so loud. A say A would test it after A leave the place, but A couldn't very well tes' it on the bus.

[JIM goes into his shoes, takes money out, give it to her.]

GLORIA: Lawd, dis husband o' mine. If nuh for his sake, den for mine, make dem good. So lock the window.

[He is in the process of doing so, when there is a knock.]
Is who dat?

JIM: A don't expect anybody. Hide the money!

[She hides it under a pillow – then sits on it. He leaves the bedroom very tentatively and goes into the living area. He looks through the peepholes at front door. He panics. He bobs and weaves back into the bedroom.]

JIM: Jesus Christ, Gloria!!

GLORIA: Is what!!!

JIM: Dem set me up!

GLORIA: Is what!!!

JIM: Police!

GLORIA: Police??!!

[JIM *and* GLORIA *are in a state of high panic.* JIM *is completely confused.*]

JIM: A whole battalion. Rass! Bring the money. Go through the back. Bury it in the back yard.

[GLORIA *is on her way there, when she sees the policemen in the back yard.*]

GLORIA: Dem round the back too, Jim. Dem surround the yard.

JIM: A will go out to dem, you go in the bathroom. Flush it!

GLORIA: But Jim…

JIM: Do what A tell yuh, Gloria. Flush it! Any place we hide it, dem will find it, so flush it!

GLORIA: But Jim…

JIM: Is jail dat…

[*Knock, knock… "Police"… from offstage.*]

JIM: Coming…!!

[GLORIA *disappears into the bathroom. A police siren is heard.* JIM *exits to the outside…* GLORIA *comes on and walks tentatively to the grill gate. Jim is entering.*]

JIM: Gloria. Gloria – yuh did what A tell yuh?

GLORIA: Yes

JIM: Jesus God!

GLORIA: What happen?

JIM: Yuh flush it?

GLORIA: Yes Jim.

JIM: Everything gone to rass!!

GLORIA: What happen? Where the police?

JIM: Them gone.

GLORIA: Say what?!

JIM: Wrong house. They had a report about a prowler at No 13 They got the numbers mixed up an come to 30 instead. Yuh flush it Gloria?

GLORIA: Yes Jim.

[JIM *is crying like a baby.*]

JIM: Yuh certain yuh flush it?

[*She nods*]

GLORIA: All gone. I know how yuh feel, but is all right at it dis way. It might have been counterfeit.

JIM: Mi whole life, Gloria.

GLORIA: On the other hand, it might have been good money... The value of the property gone up, dats all. Any time yuh sit on the seat now, yuh will be sitting on a gold mine.

JIM: Is nuh time for joke.

GLORIA: What yuh want me to do? Bawl? If A start to bawl, A won't stop.

JIM: After all the starvation; is better A did eat it.

GLORIA: It would gone down the drain same way.

JIM: We divorce for nutten Gloria. All to naught.

GLORIA: Look on the bright side, Jim. F.I.U. might have catch me at the airport...

JIM: You right... A going kill meself... A dead as it is... yuh have a piece of rope?

GLORIA: Jim, is all right, nuh fret yuhself... A never flush it...

JIM: The way things is, A can't even afford to kill miself...

GLORIA: Jim, A say A never flush it...

JIM: Say what! But how come yuh tell me...

GLORIA: Let dis be a lesson to yuh. For a man who say him is the General, you too quick to panic.

[*She goes into the bathroom and returns with the money still wrapped in its plastic. It is dripping wet, but secure.*]

JIM: After all the trouble. A only hope now say them good.

GLORIA: Is dat now – tester?

JIM: Tester! Oh!

[*He goes to where he had hidden it. He gives it to* GLORIA.]

GLORIA: Say yuh prayers.

[JIM *prays as she unwraps money and runs a note over the tester.*]

JIM: Red light!

GLORIA: Thank yuh Jesus!

JIM: Solid!

[*She tests another note.*]

GLORIA: Thank yuh Lord.

JIM: Solid Gold!

[*She tests another one.*]

GLORIA: Amen!

JIM: Is time to call Miami... We got the Onions.

[*He does a little dance. GLORIA starts to sing.*]

GLORIA: At the Cross, at the Cross...

[*She continues to test the money. JIM picks up the phone.*]

JIM: Operator? Get me Miami 305-612-6211... Charles E.
Wright... James Thomas... I'll hold.

[*GLORIA leaves the bedroom and goes toward JIM by the phone, her eyes filled with tears.*]

GLORIA: Jim, everything solid...

[*JIM extends his arm to her and encircles her with it.*]

JIM: Oh Gloria! We ready! Dis is it! Start to pack! Book yuh
ticket. Uncle Sam, we is on yuh doorstep. We gone clear.

[*JIM is talking on the telephone.*]

Hello.

[*The lights fade on them.*]

Act Two

Scene 1

[JIM *enters from the bathroom, carrying a radio. It is playing hard acid rock. He stops, switches stations. He tunes in to a Miami station.*]

ANNOUNCER: This is WINZ, Miami – under cloudy skies with a 40 percent chance of rain. It's 7:45 in the swinging city, and right now let's swing along with Glenn Miller and his orchestra "In the Mood".

   [As JIM *leaves the bedroom and goes toward the dining area, he dances to the music. Then a helicopter is heard overhead. It drowns out the radio... He goes to the window, as the helicopter lights are seen.*]

JIM: Shine yuh lights. Soldier Boy. Shine yuh light. Circle and come back. Don't forget, all right.
   [As *he waves to the departing helicoptor, he turns off the radio. It is quiet, he is restless. His eyes light on the photographs of his children.*]
   Boy, Paul, you all right? You see yuh mother up there? No? Three weeks now she leave, not a word from her. Anyway, you take care till A come up; and take care of Andrew... Tell him to work hard at school.
   [He *moves to Suzie's picture.*]
   An Suzie girl, A will make it up to yuh. We going be a family again.

39

[*He looks in the direction of Pops's room and talks at the door.*]

You going be there too, enh Pops… Answer me then, nuh. A know yuh in the house. A hear yuh last night. Ha, ha… All right, time to take a five.

[*He takes* GLORIA's *picture down, and goes to the bedroom, which is very untidy, as is the rest of the house. He talks directly to the photograph.*]

JIM: Sister Glo, yuh okay? A don't know why A can't get it out o' mi head dat something wrong.

[*He puts the photograph down on the dressing table, then tries to make the bed. He finds a pack of biscuits among the sheets. He dusts the ants away.*]

JIM: Damn ants, want bite me on mi willie nuh…

[*He eats a biscuit, then returns to the photograph. He looks at it while he sits on the bed.*]

JIM: You still look okay. What happening to me? After twenty years… Dis is madness…

[*He pauses.*]

Another Tuesday night. No.

[*Another pause.*]

Hmmmm… Mi hair drop out already as it is… Why yuh watching me so?

[*He turns her picture around. He turns the radio on and puts out the light. Music is loud and orgasmic for 10 to 15 seconds.* JIM *is in bed masturbating. Then the lights are switched on…* JIM *panics.*]

JIM: Lord ha mercy.

[*He comes up from under the sheets to see* GLORIA. *She lowers the volume on the radio.*]

GLORIA: A need 25 dollars for the taxi…

JIM: Ahm, look in mi trousers…

GLORIA: Where is it?

JIM: Ahm, over dey.

GLORIA: A don't see it.

JIM: It over dey man.

GLORIA: Jesus Christ, Jim, the taxi waiting. Get up nuh.

[*As she tries to pull the covers off him, he hangs on tight.*]

JIM: Look on the bureau.

[GLORIA *finds the money and goes out.* JIM *jumps to a sitting position, checks that* GLORIA *has gone out, then wraps the sheet around himself, gets up, checks bed for any telltale signs, and then goes to the bathroom. The stage is empty for a beat.* GLORIA *comes on in the living room, puts her suitcase down, surveys the mess.*]

GLORIA: Jim…

[*She enters the bedroom, notices her picture turned around. He enters, sheet wrapped around him.*]

JIM: Yuh come.

GLORIA: Dats all yuh have to say to me – "Yuh come"? A come home and is so yuh greet me. Yuh couldn't even get out o' the damn bed…

JIM: A was feeling chilly…

GLORIA: Chilly! Three weeks A was freezing mi ass off up dere, an' yuh tellin' me yuh was chilly.

JIM: A glad yuh come.

GLORIA: A see the proof.

JIM: What yuh say?

GLORIA: What happen? Yuh thought A was dead?

JIM: It cross mi mind, yes. A never see yuh come back, and A didn't know what happen to yuh…

GLORIA: So dat's why yuh turn mi picture around?

JIM: Picture? What? Oh dat. A was dusting, y'know cobwebbing. Oh yes, A remember now. A turn the picture to cobweb it, when A heard a knocking at the gate. A forget to turn it back…

[*He reverses it.*]

41

GLORIA: So yuh was cobwebbing?!

JIM: Yeah, man... so tell me.

GLORIA: A must say yuh did a nice job. The house really sparkling.

[*She goes into the bathroom.*]

JIM: Pshaw! Don't deal with me so.

GLORIA: Jim, man! Come here!

JIM: A know, A know. In dere stay bad.

[GLORIA *is returning to the bedroom.*]

GLORIA: Yuh don't do one thing in the house since A gone.

JIM: Forget 'bout the house nuh and tell me, how yuh do?

GLORIA: A'm okay. How you do?

JIM: A'm okay. How it went? Yuh married?

[*She shows him the ring.*]

Ha, ha, ha! An' yuh legal?

GLORIA: All the way.

JIM: Yuh really legal?

GLORIA: Yes, Jim!

JIM: Yuh hear dat, Pops. She legal! Gloria, legal...

[*He dances around... he is high as a kite. She is very low keyed.*]

What happen? Yuh don't look happy.

GLORIA: We will talk.

JIM: What happen?

GLORIA: A will talk to yuh.

[*She leaves toward the dining area.*]

JIM: Something wrong. Yuh suppose to be jumping for joy. Is what?

GLORIA: Is just dat... Well... First of all, dem search me at the airport, y'know.

JIM: Say what!?

GLORIA: Strip me stark born naked.

JIM: Jesus Christ, yuh lie...

GLORIA: Honest to God. A say, when the man take up the film. A tell him mi sister was here on holiday and forget dem, den him toss dem one side…

JIM: Wheww!!

GLORIA: Den him ask me, "Whey the onions?"

JIM: To rass! How dem know?

GLORIA: Who yuh talk to?

JIM: A never talk to nobody.

GLORIA: Yuh sure?

JIM: Positive.

GLORIA: So it got to be on the phone.

JIM: From the night A go buy the money, A had an uneasy feeling that dem had me under wraps. So what yuh say?

GLORIA: A bluff him. A say "What onions? So much onions in Miami, what A carrying onion up there for?" Him look on me an say "Go on."

[JIM *hisses*.]

JIM: Damn little F.I.U. bwoy dem; think dem can match wits wid me. Dem is amateur! What A tell yuh, Gloria, I is the General. Dem could search till thy kingdom come, dem would never find where I put dat money…

GLORIA: Whey YOU put it?! Nuh me come up with the idea? An stop dat nonsense bout yuh is the General, General mi ass!

JIM: Why yuh getting so hot under the collar?

GLORIA: I take all the risk!

JIM: Okay, okay, yuh good too…

GLORIA: Good too!! Why it so hard for yuh to admit dat A worth something?!

JIM: A was running a little joke…

GLORIA: Joke?!! A know yuh!! Now A go an come back yuh can say anything… bout yuh is the General. So is you mastermind it for them to search me at the airport, an make me miss mi plane?

JIM: You miss the plane?

GLORIA: So when A reach Miami, the man wasn't dere to meet me.

JIM: So what yuh do, Gloria?

GLORIA: A phone him number 'bout ten times. No answer.

JIM: Jesus!

GLORIA: A took stock o' mi situation. A had to find a place to sleep. Dem had a hotel in the airport, but when dem tell me the price, A say no.

JIM: How much so?

GLORIA: Sixty dollars U.S., plus tax.

JIM: For the week...

GLORIA: For the night!

JIM: At the rate A buy the money?!! Blouse beat! So what yuh do Gloria?

GLORIA: A decide to sit it out at the airport. Den a next panic lick me. Is Friday A go up. Suppose the man don't work again till Monday?

JIM: Him work on Saturday, Gloria?

GLORIA: Wait nuh, Jim.

JIM: Don't keep me in suspense, man...

[GLORIA *begins to re-enact the events in Miami.*]

GLORIA: A take up a seat, lap mi foot over the suitcase, and clutch mi handbag. A watch the time. A get up and A walk; A walk; A tired; A doze off; A wake up.

JIM: Him work Saturday, Gloria?

GLORIA: A wake up an' see two suspicious looking white bwoy eyeing me. A clutch mi handbag.

JIM: Cuban dem nuh!

GLORIA: A wouldn't know if dem was Cuban, Jim; but A couldn't sleep out there. A had to go bathroom an it come to me dat in there would be the safest place to sleep.

[JIM *turns up his nose.*]

So A nap, and suddenly A wake up, and when A look under the door, A see a shoes. Something never right 'bout dem shoes. Den it hit me! It was a man shoes.

JIM: Is in the man toilet yuh go sleep, Gloria?

GLORIA: A draw up myself in a little ball, tight, tight…
[*She enacts it.*]
And A pray. The shoes don't move. Den A see when him hand come down, den piece o' him head.

JIM: Him checking if yuh in dey!

GLORIA: A tighten up myself even more. Him couldn't see me. Few seconds later, him walk 'way. A listen for the door, den A fly out… Outside A see one o' the white bwoy dat was eyeing mi handbag, and when A look on him shoes…

JIM: The same Cuban bwoy…

GLORIA: The same shoes…

JIM: Is Cuban definitely. Yuh can always tell a Cuban by him shoes.

GLORIA: A walk up and down all night.

JIM: Him work Saturday, Gloria?

GLORIA: Yes. Him work Saturday.

JIM: Problem solved!

GLORIA: Dats what you think. A had to find mi way up dey. Him give me one set o' directions – north, west, den go east on 177, an' all dem kinda thing. A couldn't make head nor tail o' the directions.

JIM: Is so Uncle Sam scientific – none o' dis turn right, turn left business.

GLORIA: Well, is the turn right, turn left business A accustomed to. So by the time A reach outside the airport is lost A lost.

JIM: Den yuh nuh catch yuh directions off the sun, Baby. It rise in the west, set in the east; north, south.

GLORIA: It rise in the *east* Jim…

JIM: Is so? You have to be nautical…

45

GLORIA: Yuh can chat. Yuh wasn't up dey. A porter carry mi little suitcase couple feet, an when him put it down him say, "You won't see me again." So A tell him "Ba bye." The man say…
   [*She speaks louder.*]
   "You won't see me again"… so A look on him, and he shove him hand under mi nose an say, "You can tip me now!" So a give him a dollar.

JIM: Is the system, Gloria. Uncle Sam organize it dat everybody can make a buck.

GLORIA: A had to take two bus…

JIM: Yuh ride on the luxury bus, Gloria? Dem nice, enh!

GLORIA: Not the one I ride on to Liberty City. A sit down on the tough seat an watch the fancy tall building with the white people get lower an lower, till dem reach shack with black people, an' A was in the heart of the ghetto.

JIM: Gloria, yuh sure is America yuh go?

GLORIA: Yes Jim. A was up dey. An A come off the bus, and had to walk 'mongst the pushers, the winos, an' the addicts. All eyes on me! A nuh little guard. A guard mi handbag…

JIM: If dat damn Jamaican from Catadupa did pick yuh at the airport, all dat wouldn't happen to yuh.

GLORIA: A glad him never come Jim. A learn 'bout the place. A don't think A would ever forget. A stop at a furniture factory to ask directions, an' as A approach, a white man say, "What yuh want?" so A show him the piece of paper with the address, an' him say, "We don't give directions – GET LOST!" An' A hear him say to him friend, "Nigger…"

JIM: What!!! Who him talking to? Who him calling Nigger? So what yuh do? Yuh didn't kick him in him… Yuh have him address? Yuh wait till A get up there.

GLORIA: The eye water roll down mi face, as A head back out in the rain an' stop a taxi.

JIM: Is the South – we don't have to go there…

46

GLORIA: The taxi man drive me round an' round, an' after 'bout ten minutes him let me off in front o' the building, which was right round the corner from the furniture factory.

JIM: Damn t'ief. Dat happen all over the world all the same…

GLORIA: A walk up the stairs to the consultant place, an' A say to miself "Lord whey A going?" Yuh see the fancy card the man give me, Suite 1-2-3! Is a little dutty place wid one typewriter an' a fish tank wid a dead fish. Him take me to some dingy little apartment, an' tell me the wedding was in a few days time. A jam something behind the door an' try to sleep. I hear gunshot same way.

JIM: Up dey?

GLORIA: An' siren keeping me awake all night.
   [*Shots*]

JIM: Lock up the house.
   [JIM *secures the bolts, etc. in the living room.* GLORIA *lifts suitcase into the bedroom. Then he follows her.*]

GLORIA: I am home! Boy, Jim. A am having some serious reservation 'bout this America thing, y'know.

JIM: Say what? Reser… what? Gloria, A don't say yuh didn't have one or two bad experience, but as A say…

GLORIA: Jim, even the man A married think A would be an ass to leave what A have here, an' him is a native. Him take me round an' show me…

JIM: Wait a minute, Gloria. Yuh an' dis man chat? A think yuh jus' see him, marry him, an' leave him. How come him taking yuh 'round?

GLORIA: We had to live together Jim… Jim. Jim – don't jump to conclusions, let me tell yuh how it went. It was the consultant who insist we stay together. Dere's dis interview before yuh get yuh residency papers, an' we had to be prepared for it. Is to make sure yuh don't get married just to get the US visa, like the Immigration man suggest I do. A

47

had to look him straight in the eye an' say, "Sir, I got married for love." I was in one room, an mi husband in the other, an' is one intimate question after another... like what colour nighties A wear to bed last night. At the same time dem cross check an' ask the man the same question.

JIM: Him sleep dey Gloria?

GLORIA: Yes Jim. On the couch.

JIM: Him try anything Gloria?

GLORIA: No Jim...

JIM: Him rape yuh Gloria?

GLORIA: A say No Jim.

JIM: Him never had to rape yuh. All him had to do was demand him legal rights. Him rape yuh Gloria?

GLORIA: No Jim.

JIM: Yuh fight him off...

GLORIA: Dere was no need to. Him never try anything.

JIM: Yuh can't scream. Yuh can't call Police. What yuh do Gloria?

GLORIA: Jim. A say the man never try anything.

JIM: Him never even ask for a little cheups?
    [*Makes the sound of a kiss.*]

GLORIA: No.

JIM: Is a miracle! The man yuh married is either a angel, a battyman or a cripple.

GLORIA: I wouldn't know, Jim.

JIM: Is what kinda man dis man?

GLORIA: Who, Johnny?

JIM: Johnny? Johnny what him name?

GLORIA: Johnny Peters the Third.

JIM: So yuh is...

GLORIA: For the time being, Jim.

JIM: What him look like?

GLORIA: Black, fortyish, sorta resemble Pops in him younger days.

JIM: Pops was a good-looking man. What him do up dey?

GLORIA: Him is a animal control officer.

JIM: Say what?

GLORIA: A dog catcher, Jim…

JIM: Gloria, yuh serious?

GLORIA: Nutten wrong wid it. Job is job…

JIM: Him would do well down here… Him could catch flea for all A care. Him serve him purpose. Thank yuh Lord. It is all over. When A think o' what we go through. Is a high price we pay for dat visa.

GLORIA: A don't think it worth the price, Jim. Is two America. White America, Black America. Which one yuh going to? A check out a lot o' things up dere – job, housing. At least we don't owe nutten on dis.

JIM: Gloria, we gone too far. We can't turn back now. A have a man coming to buy the house. Gloria, yuh forget we not doing dis for weself… Pops sacrifice him life so dat we could be wid the children…

GLORIA: Jim, maybe we read him wrong…

JIM: Gloria, yuh chatting nonsense…

GLORIA: Don't tell me dat again, Jim!

[*She shouts at him.*]

JIM: What come over yuh woman?

GLORIA: A'm tell yuh how A feel, an' what A think, an' yuh call it nonsense. Maybe what Pops was saying is, dat is time yuh stop treating me like shit!

JIM: Gloria!!!

GLORIA: A tell yuh what Jim. Is minimum six months before we can go up dey, so we have time to think 'bout it.

JIM: Gloria…

GLORIA: Make it rest for now…

JIM: Cool…

GLORIA: Okay.

[JIM *makes another attempt to discuss the matter.*]

Jim!!

JIM: I did all buy a bottle o' Wincarnis to celebrate. I might as well drink it.

[*He is going towards the dining area.*]

GLORIA: Pour me a little.

[JIM *is amazed that* GLORIA *has made a demand of him. He stops and returns to the bedroom to reassert his position of authority.*]

JIM: All the glasses dutty. Go wash two, a' while yuh in the kitchen, fix me something nice to eat, A sorta peckish. A haven't had a decent meal since yuh leave.

GLORIA: Yuh little people never feed yuh!

JIM: Yuh come back wid dat nonsense Gloria. Look how mi hand burn up.

[*She looks at it.*]

A was trying to light the stove.

[*She looks at him blankly.*]

Yuh shoulda seen it the first day.

GLORIA: Yuh poor thing…

JIM: It almost burn down the house.

GLORIA: Hmm…

JIM: Bread outside. Just rustle up something nice to put in between it…

GLORIA: Not tonight, Jim…

JIM: Come nuh, sweetness…

[*He gets physical in an attempt to sweeten her up.*]

GLORIA: Nuh bother.

[*She pushes him off.*]

JIM: Come nuh, man. A really hungry, yuh know. A will go try light the stove…

[*He goes out.*]

50

GLORIA: If yuh think I going into dat dutty kitchen tonight, yuh have anodder guess coming!!

[JIM *stops in the dining room when he realizes that* GLORIA *is not following him.*]

JIM: Gloria!

GLORIA: Yes, Jim.

JIM: Come here.

GLORIA: If yuh want me, come to me...

JIM: No man! Yuh come!

[*He tries to reassert his dominance.*]

GLORIA: Stay out there then.

[JIM *returns to the bedroom area and sees her in a state of half undress.*]

JIM: Gloria, what game yuh playing wid me tonight? Come here to me an' stop yuh nonsense...

[*He tries a little sexual blackmail.*]

GLORIA: No, Jim. No!

[*He continues his assault.*]

A will scream!

JIM: Scream then.

[*She screams.*]

Yuh mad woman!!!

GLORIA: Take what A say serious, Jim. When A say "No," A mean no...

JIM: What happen to yuh?

GLORIA: Right now, we not married, y'know...

JIM: So?

GLORIA: So don't take anyting for granted. Look now. If yuh serious 'bout going to America, we going have to remarry, but before we do dat, yuh going have to court me again.

JIM: But is what yuh come back wid. What yuh say? Court yuh? Court yuh how?

GLORIA: You know. Yuh did it before…

[JIM *falls on his knees.*]

JIM: Oh Gloria, Victoria, h'apple of my h'eye, love of mi life…

GLORIA: What yuh say yuh doing?

JIM: Yuh say A must court yuh.

GLORIA: A serious, yuh know. A'm not going back into it under the same conditions. Dere's going have to be a new understanding. All dem things like "Feed me"… whether A sick, A dying, or just come off the plane, "Feed me"…

JIM: A think yuh woulda been happy to do something for me, after all is three weeks…

GLORIA: Jim, is twenty years o' "Feed me." "Feed me" is done!

JIM: Feed me dis one last time…

GLORIA: Yuh think A joking.

[*Pause*]

JIM: All right den. Come we go to bed.

GLORIA: Yuh think *dat* will make me change mi mind. Y'know what, A going sleep in Pops's room…

JIM: Gloria…

GLORIA: From now on regard me as a guest, an' A expect yuh to treat yuh guest accordingly. If yuh really serious 'bout marrying me again, yuh can start by cleaning up the house, a' washing up the dutty dishes. See yuh in the morning. An' A plan to lock the door.

[*She goes.*]

JIM: What the ASS. Mi marriage mash up over a sandwich?

[BLACKOUT]

Act Two, Scene 2

[*It is the following day. The lights come up on* JIM *making the bed, fluffing out the pillows and doing it very well. He picks up* GLORIA's *shoes, mutters under his breath about having to do woman's work. He leaves the bedroom, taking the radio with him, and puts it on the shelf in the dining area. The dining table is a mess of dirty plates, etc.* JIM *looks at them maliciously, collects them and exits to the kitchen off stage. A few moments pass, then the sound of plates breaking. Soon after,* JIM *returns to the dining area with four plates. He is about to smash another when he hears* GLORIA *coming.*]

JIM: Bitch!

[*He puts the plates away quickly as* GLORIA *enters through the front door.*]

GLORIA: What's happening?

JIM: I am here.

[GLORIA *goes into the kitchen.* JIM *watches her. He waits for her outburst over the broken plates.* GLORIA *returns, says nothing, and is going to the bedroom.*]

JIM: Yuh have a *Star?*

[*She give it to him and continues toward the bedroom.* JIM *watches her, uncertain; then he follows her.*]

All right! Cuss me. Get it over with.

GLORIA: Cuss yuh? What for?

JIM: 'Bout the plates.

GLORIA: A muss cus' yuh, Jim?

JIM: Is some o' yuh best crockery. I know dat.

GLORIA: Them was yuh wedding present as much as mine. How much yuh bruck?

JIM: Yuh mean how much drop out o' mi hand an' bruck ... Six ...

53

GLORIA: Is okay. A wouldn't worry 'bout it.

JIM: A thought yuh woulda been mad.

[*He returns to the dining table.*]

GLORIA: No. Practice make perfect. If yuh have to bruck all o' dem, so be it. Yuh have to learn …

[*Pause*]

JIM: So Gloria …

GLORIA: Yes, Jim …

JIM: What yuh doing out on the street till now?

GLORIA: A guess A better warn yuh. A'm starting evening classes at St John's College … three evenings a week.

JIM: When yuh decide dat?

GLORIA: Is something A always wanted to do.

JIM: Yuh could at least have discussed it with me.

GLORIA: A did – years ago …

JIM: Say what?

GLORIA: Guess yuh don't remember what yuh say to me …

JIM: No. Remind me.

GLORIA: "So who will look after the children?" Well the children not here, and Pops gone, so – classes run 5.30 to 7.30.

JIM: What kinda classes?

GLORIA: I am planning to be a nurse …

JIM: At your age? I hear 'bout Florence Nightingale, but what yuh planning to be – Florence Fowl?

[GLORIA *looks at him, then goes to the dining area.*]

So who will look after mi food when I come home hungry at night?

GLORIA: Yuh will have to learn to fend for yuhself in the kitchen; so yuh better come watch what A doin'…

JIM: A don't understand yuh. Yuh leave here a perfectly normal good woman, yuh go to America for three weeks, and yuh come back with all dem corrupt new-fangle ideas. Who influence yuh?

GLORIA: A have a mind of mi own. Why yuh think somebody have to influence me?

JIM: But must. Is not so yuh leave here.

GLORIA: Same person go, same person come.

JIM: No sir!

GLORIA: A just never confident myself to talk to yuh before, an' insist dat yuh listen to me.

JIM: Gloria, A don't understand what's going on. First yuh want me to wash plate, now yuh want me to cook, an' dis thing 'bout going to school! What happen, we not going to 'Merica?

GLORIA: I not qualified for anything, yuh know. An if A go to America – IF – we don't decide yet – A not going up there to clean white people floor. So A determined to go to school. But right now I need yuh help …

JIM: Why all the changes?

GLORIA: A not asking for much …

[JIM *hisses his teeth.*]

Why yuh have to be so discouraging? For once in yuh life, help me to do something for ME nuh man … Come nuh man … A will show yuh what to do.

[*There is a long pause as* JIM *ponders his decision.*]

JIM: What yuh cooking?

GLORIA: Mince. Yuh can wash the rice.

JIM: Pass the soap.

GLORIA: To do what?

JIM: Wash the rice.

GLORIA: Sometimes A wonder if yuh really have sense. Catch some water. I will show yuh.

[JIM *goes off to get the water, as she gets the rice. He returns.*]

JIM: Uncle Ben's. Yuh bring dis back with yuh?

GLORIA: Yes. Measure it out. One cup to two cups water.

JIM: Dis is the real thing. The Rolls Royce of Rice. Genuine American. This can eat by itself.

[*They measure.*]

Is years A don't do this.

GLORIA: Yuh use to cook?

JIM: When A was a little boy go to spend time in the country. A use to cook in the bush.

GLORIA: So how come yuh can't cook rice?

[*Goes off with rice to kitchen.*]

JIM: Rice was a luxury in dem days. Is banana, breadfruit, yampi A use to deal with. Cook up with salt pork in a kerosene pan... den yuh eat it out banana leaf. Sweet!

GLORIA: Yuh have to give me the recipe.

JIM: How much salt?

GLORIA: Do yuh thing, man.

[*He finds the salt, sprinkles the food, then throws some over his shoulders.*]

JIM: Cool. Where the *Onions.*

[*They laugh at his reference. She gets it from the refrigerator and gives it to him.*]

Is Uncle Sam feeding us.

GLORIA: Is our fault dat.

JIM: Black pepper.

[*He sprinkles generously.*]

Is not bad fun...

GLORIA: Is the first time we ever do anything together.

JIM: Dat not true, Gloria.

GLORIA: Apart from *dat...*

JIM: No. Yuh remember when we was courting?

[*He laughs.*]

All the times A took yuh to play cricket with the boys?

GLORIA: It was my job to field.

[JIM *stops cooking and picks up an object which he uses as a bat and goes through the motion of playing strokes.*]

JIM: An' yuh wasn't a bad fielder, for a woman…

GLORIA: A never get a chance to bat, though…

JIM: How yuh mean? Woman can't bat!

GLORIA: Yuh never try me.

JIM: Yuh really wanted to bat?

GLORIA: Yes.

JIM: Why yuh didn't say so?

GLORIA: And what yuh would say – "GLORIA, GO FIELD!"

JIM: An' after the game, we would go traipsing through Race Course hand in hand, an yuh would look on me with yuh goat eye…

GLORIA: Mi one regret, 'bout dem days, is we never sit down an' chat.

JIM: Say we never chat…

GLORIA: We chat yes, but we never discuss what we wanted out of life; what we wanted out of the marriage. We never really get to know each other, Jim …

JIM: The only way we never get to know each other was in the Biblical way. Nuh true? All the time the Parson was saying the vows, is one thing was on mi mind.
[*He tries to caress her.*]

GLORIA: A know dat. Behave yuhself, Jim.

JIM: Exact same thing yuh use to say. "Behave yuhself, Jim."
[*He touches her again.*]

GLORIA: Don't do dat …

JIM: Yuh hold out on me bad, y'know. Oh boy. A will never forget the first time. What a night dat was. You remember it, Gloria?
[*JIM's face is alive with pleasurable memories, while GLORIA's reflects her bad times.*]

Oh boy. Hmmm, it was worth waiting for. Still is. But Gloria,
all the times yuh tell me no, yuh didn't want to do it too?

GLORIA: What yuh think?

JIM: Dat no. A know yuh as a woman of principle. Nuh so?

GLORIA: No.

JIM: How yuh mean no. Yuh wanted to do it before we married?

GLORIA: Wanted to do it, yes.

JIM: 'Onest!?

GLORIA: It was a serious thing…

JIM: Is so? So what yuh do? Take a cold shower?

GLORIA: Well…

[She laughs.]

What yuh do, Jim?

JIM: Go for a ride on mi bicycle. What yuh do?

GLORIA: Why yuh want to know?

JIM: A just curious.

GLORIA: A will tell yuh…

JIM: Now, man…

GLORIA: A soon come.

[She goes into the kitchen.]

JIM: Gloria, come here.

GLORIA: What?

JIM: What yuh use to do?

GLORIA: A will whisper an' tell yuh …

JIM: Why yuh can't say it out loud?

GLORIA: A just   …

JIM: All right! Whisper!

[She goes up to him and whispers.]

A didn't hear yuh. Come again.

[She whispers in his ear for the second time.]

Gloria, yuh really do dat?

GLORIA: A know A shouldn't tell yuh …

JIM: Woman don't do dem things …

58

GLORIA: Yuh do it, though…

JIM: Me? Yuh must be crazy. Yuh think I want hair grow in mi hand middle?

[*He looks at his palm – then double takes.*]

It nuh right … A guess if it was before we married. But since den yuh been getting the real thing, enh? Enh Gloria?

GLORIA: Aye, Jim …

JIM: What yuh mean by dat? Yuh do it since, Gloria? A ask yuh a question. Yuh do it since we married?

GLORIA: Yes, Jim?!

JIM: Yes yuh answer me, or yes yuh do it?

GLORIA: Yes. A do it!

[*There is a long pause. JIM is stunned. He looks away, then directly at her. Then looks off again. Hisses. There is a silence. She goes to the bathroom.*]

JIM: The woman leave the bridal suite, leave me, to go do dat!

[*His eyes light on a tin of Baygon spray. He picks it up and goes after her.*]

Gloria, show me mi competition. Show me!!

GLORIA: Why yuh behaving so? At leas' A never go outside an look for a man.

JIM: Is better if yuh do dat. What yuh do nuh natural. What yuh use?

GLORIA: Jim, stop questioning me…

JIM: Yuh tell me say yuh do it. Yuh might as well tell me what yuh use.

GLORIA: It was in the bathroom, Jim.

JIM: With what?

GLORIA: With the water.

JIM: The water? Them things I read bout in dutty book, you introduce into mi yard? Jesus Christ. Is nuh one or two times the Water Commission come check the meter. Nutten wrong with it. Now I know!

GLORIA: Why yuh behaving so? Yuh was thinking 'bout it during the marriage ceremony. Me was thinking 'bout it too. Only trouble is, what A did expect an' what A get was two different things. Is like YOU reach where YOU was going, while I still going up the hill...

JIM: What yuh saying to me? Say dat A don't satisfy yuh?

[*Pause*]

Is five times yuh breed. How yuh mean A don't satisfy yuh?

GLORIA: All A'm saying is dat when yuh gone leave me, A had to carry miself over the hill.

JIM: To rass!

GLORIA: At first A thought something was wrong with me...

JIM: But must ...

GLORIA: Yuh see what A mean. Yuh see why A could never talk to yuh 'bout it.

JIM: Say me nuh satisfy yuh. After me all jack yuh up wid twins ...

GLORIA: Because A breed, it nuh mean A satisfy ...

JIM: Something wrong wid yuh ...

GLORIA: Nutten wrong wid me.

JIM: Jesus Christ woman. How many times yuh tell me how yuh enjoy yuhself wid me? So what yuh coming wid now?

GLORIA: A never volunteer the information. Is yuh ask me.

JIM: An' what yuh say?

[*The following two speeches are spoken at the same time.*]

GLORIA: A never want to hurt yuh feelings, Jim. If yuh was happy, A was happy. But after a while A say to miself, "But Jim not thinking 'bout me, him only thinking 'bout him damn self." So A had to do something for me. An' all dem times when yuh was out wid yuh little sweetheart, an' come back cock sure o' yuhself an don't need me, I done make certain dat A don't need yuh either.

JIM: How yuh could defile yuhself so? A woman body is her temple, the altar of her shrine. Yuh risk madhouse for self gratification? Yuh hair could o' drop out. Imagine me married to a bald head woman. Nice quiet Gloria! An' all the time I think 'bout yuh as the little lady I married. Nice quiet Gloria, mi ass! An all dat shit bout wash plate! A should o' bruck the whole lot o' dem! A going down the road ... A must find somebody NORMAL to deal wid ...

GLORIA: A don't understand yuh. Yuh can't manage yuh homework properly, yet yuh taking on extracurricular activity...

JIM: Put it dis way, I can't compete with Niagara Falls!

[*He goes across and throws her picture down. JIM exits. GLORIA stops for a moment, then goes to her handbag. She takes out a piece of paper, goes to the phone and dials 113.*]

GLORIA: Operator. Calling Miami 305-595-5941, to speak to Mr Johnny Peters the Third. Calling from 92 28461. My name? Mrs Johnny Peters the Third.

[BLACKOUT]

Act Two, Scene 3

[*The lights go up on GLORIA packing. A knocking is heard at the front door. GLORIA leaves her packing, looks through the peephole at the front door to the outside, and sees JIM. In his hurry at the end of the previous scene, he forgot to take his key. She opens the door and leaves immediately for the bedroom area. JIM enters and sits at the dining table.*]

JIM: Gloria...
GLORIA: What?

JIM: Come here.

GLORIA: For what?

JIM: A want to say something to yuh.

GLORIA: What about?

JIM: A sorry 'bout what happen dis evening.

GLORIA: Me, too.

JIM: A come to a decision.

GLORIA: Me, too.

JIM: Gloria, A going try an' deal with it.

GLORIA: Deal with what?

JIM: Yuh an' dat thing.

[GLORIA *comes into the dining area.*]

GLORIA: What thing?

JIM: The thing dat cause the friction between us.

GLORIA: There has always been friction between us. The only way dere will ever be peace is if I shut mi mouth, an I done bite mi tongue an' swallow mi spit.

JIM: Gloria …

GLORIA: Dat thing! Yuh can't even bring yuhself to say it! So how yuh going deal with it?

JIM: A go deep into miself, an' come to certain realizations. None of us is perfect…

GLORIA: An yuh more perfect than me. In fact, A am the perfect fart.

[*leaves for the bedroom.*]

JIM: A didn't mean it so …

GLORIA: So how yuh mean it den? 'Bout none of us is perfect?

[GLORIA *goes into the bathroom. JIM follows her to the bedroom. He sees her packing.*]

JIM: What yuh doing? Where yuh going?

[GLORIA *returns from the bathroom and tosses some toilet articles into the suitcase.*]

Is not enough dat A say A will try an' deal with it?

GLORIA: No. Is not enough. Yuh can't deal wid something yuh don't understand. Dat yuh not even willing to try an' understand. Every time A go bathroom, yuh go wonder is what A up to inside dere. An every time the water bill come, yuh go wonder how it so high …

JIM: Don't bring it up again. A willing to forget it.

GLORIA: Is so yuh planning to deal wid it, by forgetting it?! No, Jim, all it will do is stay under the surface an' fester.

JIM: Gloria, A not letting yuh go!

GLORIA: Why, not, Jim?

JIM: Yuh belong to me.

GLORIA: A'm not yuh property to lend, lease, or rent. Yuh selfishness in the bed is just the tip of the iceberg. In every other area o' we life is the same thing. Yuh too damn selfish. An' dat is what yuh have to deal with. Yuh selfishness.

JIM: Is not one or two sacrifice A make for yuh an' the family? Every farthing A ever earn come into dis house.

GLORIA: Dat is not enough. Every farthing I ever earn come in here too. Money is not the problem. What yuh ever give of yuhself? When yuh ever do something yuh don't want to do, dat will put yuh out of yuh way, enh? Apart from yuh selfishness, yuh is a vindictive an' destructive man. Why yuh mash the plates?

JIM: A will buy dem back, Gloria…

GLORIA: They can't replace …

[*She leaves the bedroom to go to the kitchen area to collect the remaining plates. He goes after her.*]

Why Jim? Coz yuh know dem is dear to me. Is a wicked act. Anyhow, it don't matter now. Is years now yuh beat me into submission an' try to make me feel dat A not up to much, coz yuh had to feel yuh was General King Kong. Putting me on the plane was the best thing yuh ever do for me. Every time A come up 'gainst a obstacle, A find a way 'round it.

[*She brushes past* JIM *as she leaves the dining area and returns to the bedroom.*]

If A can deal with life on an international level why A should make yuh subject me to be nutten but a damn dishwasher. A finish wid dat – so between now an' when A leave …

JIM: Gloria, we go through too much together to end up like dis. Think 'bout the children. What about Pops's sacrifice? Yuh can't walk out just so …

GLORIA: Dat idea yuh have 'bout Pops sacrificing himself for the children nutten like dat. When yuh lay down the law dat the children must go up dere, get lost, don't communicate, I discuss it wid Pops. An' Pops agree dat we couldn't abandon the children. Read dis –

[*She gives him a letter.*]

Read it.

[JIM *starts to read.*]

JIM: Rub a dub dub, three men in a tub… What kind o' nonsense is dis?

GLORIA: Is a letter from Suzie. Pops help we work out the code. Dat tell me dat she living with a family an' she hoping to do Computer Programming.

JIM: Dis?

GLORIA: Dat! Yuh read Pops wrong. Him knew all along where the children was, an' what was happening to dem. Yuh can't use the children or Pops as an excuse any longer…

JIM: A don't understand. Mi old man conspire 'gainst me. If yuh know all dis time, why we go through all the distress, the starvation to get the visa?

GLORIA: A had a dream 'bout America, so when yuh start to see it my way, A jump at the chance. A wanted to see mi children again. A still want to see dem, but as Pops say the night him dead … "The children going to be all right."

JIM: A worse don't understand… Pops kill himself for nutten.

64

GLORIA: No Jim. Him thank me the night for all the years o' looking after him, an' then him say "Is time now for you an' Jim to look after each other." What Pops do was clear the space so we can deal with each other, an' find weself. As long as him was in the house, we would depend on him for everything. America won't solve we problems, whether we go, or whether we stay, until we start to look into weself a' learn to help each other. Then we must expect to fail. All dat ever held us together was crisis, Jim. The greater the crisis, the closer we was. The crisis over, Jim. Is yuh an' me now. The problem is between us; an' A know yuh won't change, an' yuh won't compromise. So let me know if yuh still want to go to America. I will get yuh up. A owe yuh dat much. A will get my divorce and A will marry yuh again. It will be a business marriage, so yuh will sign a document agreeing to a divorce …

JIM: And if A don't sign it.

GLORIA: Is up to you, Jim.

[*The lights go down on them.*]

Act Two, Scene 4

[GLORIA *is in the bedroom writing a note.*]

GLORIA: "Dear Jim, There is something I didn't have a chance to tell yuh. I hope you don't misunderstand, so I will start at the beginning …
[*She stops, looks up.*]
Where do I begin?
[JIM *enters.*]

65

JIM: Gloria – you bitch, where yuh is?

[GLORIA *crumples the note*.]

Yuh never hear me calling yuh?

GLORIA: What is it Jim?

JIM: Yuh cunning little bitch!

GLORIA: Let me get outa dis house.

[*She goes to the phone and dials*.]

JIM: You do me dat? YOU woman … After twenty years … Jesus God Gloria … Yuh play me for an ass, a damn ginny … Yuh betray me… Man kill woman for less!

[GLORIA *speaks into the telephone*.]

GLORIA: Send a taxi for me to …

[JIM *snatches the phone*.]

JIM: Yuh not leaving till yuh tell me the reason why yuh leaving me.

GLORIA: A tell yuh already.

[*She is going*.]

JIM: Siddown.

GLORIA: Let me leave in peace, nuh man.

JIM: Last night, after A leave the house …

GLORIA: Oh Jesus…

JIM: Him can't help yuh now. Only the truth can set yuh free. What yuh do last night after A leave the house? Who yuh call?

[*Pause*]

Who yuh call Gloria?

[*Pause*]

Cat bite yuh tongue bitch!?!

[*She exits to the bedroom*.]

Operator – overseas? Get me Miami – 305-595-5941…

GLORIA: Jim …

[*She comes rushing back*.]

JIM: A want to talk to a Mr Johnny A Dog Catcher. Yes, Operator, yuh heard right… Dog Catcher! Dat's the name …

GLORIA: Jim. Please.

JIM: Calling on behalf of his wife, Mrs Johnny A Cornflakes Dog Catcher the Third...

GLORIA: Jim, leave him out of it ...

JIM: Move bitch! Play me for a ASS - 'bout yuh don't want to go to America ...

GLORIA: It have nutten to do wid him ...

JIM: What yuh do last night after A leave the house?

GLORIA: A call the man, Jim.

[JIM *hangs up.*]

GLORIA: A was writing you a letter to explain ...

[*She gives him the crumpled note. He takes it, looks at it, tosses it away.*]

JIM: Explain...

[*He produces a tape.*]

I Watergate yuh ass. A tell yuh don't talk on the phone. A have it as dem say – verbatim, word for word.

[*He reels off the tape, speaking pseudo-American.*]

"Gloria mah Babes – A was here just dozing off and mah mind was right on yuh. Yuh made mah day, and now to hear yuh call. Yuh make mah night complete..." Yuh want me to go on Gloria?

[*Pause*]

What A tell yuh – A is the General! Yuh believe me now? Don't trifle with the General – Babes...!

GLORIA: I know it look a way, but nothin' happen.

JIM: Yuh lie Gloria. The Yankee man screw yuh.

GLORIA: No...

JIM: The man take mi fifteen hundred dollar an' screw yuh on top o' it ...

GLORIA: Him never take the money.

[*Pause*]

JIM: Say what!! Him didn't take the money?!

67

GLORIA: Jim, let me explain it to yuh.

JIM: What yuh saying to me? What kinda love is dis? So where is the money?

GLORIA: A lodge it in Miami, so we would have a start…

JIM: We? We who?

GLORIA: Me and yuh, Jim.

JIM: Me and yuh? Yuh mean yuh and the Dogcatcher…

GLORIA: No, yuh and me…

JIM: Bankbook.

[*Holds his hands out for it.*]

GLORIA: It in Miami …

JIM: With who?

[*Pause*]

GLORIA: With him …

JIM: What yuh saying to me? The dogcatcher strikes again …

GLORIA: A couldn't very well bring it back …

JIM: Yuh is a legal U.S. citizen. Yuh don't have to hide. If A never come back today, yuh would be gone an not a word to me… Half o'dat money is mine.

GLORIA: If A wanted to carry yuh down A wouldn't come back … What A come back for, to tell yuh A gone again?

JIM: Yuh come back for yuh things. Say yuh don't want to go to America. Yuh mean yuh don't want me to, coz yuh have yuh man up dey…

GLORIA: Jim, yuh don't understand …

JIM: No, A don't understand. Worse, A don't understand how it get to "Gloria, mah Babes."

GLORIA: Jim … Yuh don't listen to me… A meet the man… A say hello, A say I do, an' dat was supposed to be dat. It wasn't my choice dat me an the man had to stay together. Is not little cuss A cuss yuh …

JIM: Cuss me?

GLORIA: Yes. A cuss yuh for putting me in dat position where A was completely at the mercy o' the man. A cuss yuh because yuh put *me* out in front to do the dutty work.

JIM: What's dat go' to do wid him calling yah "Babes"?

GLORIA: A expect the worse an' A get the bes'. The man treat me like a lady. Him don't even know me. Him put himself out o' him way to put me at ease, an' to help me, an' him never expect anything in return. A was suspicious o' the man, A wonder what him want. The only man A had to judge him off was you, an' from you who A expect the best, A get the worst!

JIM: Go to yuh man, Gloria, A don't want to hear no more.

GLORIA: You going to listen to me Jim, just like how the man listen to me. Him listen to me an' him respect mi opinion, an' not once him say A chat nonsense! Yes, Jim, him call me "Babes," because him like me… but him respect mi wishes, coz A can't deal wid more dan one at a time, so A come back to try and sort it out.

JIM: Nutten to sort out Gloria. Call the taxi, go 'bout yuh business. But before yuh go, dere is a score A have to settle with yuh.

GLORIA: A will get your half o' the money to yuh.

JIM: Is not money I dealing wid. Is *you*. Yuh say I never satisfy yuh… Well A want one more shot.

[*He grabs her, and throws her down on the bed.*]

GLORIA: Jim…!

JIM: Yes Gloria, A deserve a last try, an yuh can scream down the house…

[*JIM pins GLORIA down on the bed with his weight and attempts to undress her and himself at the same time. GLORIA lies motionless and limp on the bed. JIM is turned off by her unresponsiveness. She neither fights nor accepts. He stops, gets off her and turns away defeated.*]

JIM: Is okay, Gloria. Go catch yuh plane …

[GLORIA *sits up on the bed.*]

GLORIA: Jim …

JIM: The quicker yuh go Gloria, the better.

[GLORIA *gets up off the bed.*]

GLORIA: Jim …

JIM: Yes.

[*He answers sharply and vehemently.*]

GLORIA: All A wanted was a little reassurance from you. A was
longing to see yuh, but the night A come back, all A get was
…

[*She picks up her handbag and turns to leave the bedroom.*]

JIM: A was glad to see yuh, Gloria …

GLORIA: Yuh never show it Jim…

JIM: Is so life go sometimes …

[JIM *is silent.* GLORIA *turns to go, when* JIM *again stops
her.*]

JIM: A couldn't get out o' the bed Gloria … because…

GLORIA: A know, yuh tell me…

JIM: No. A couldn't get out because… because… because A
was doing dat t'ing.

GLORIA: What t'ing? Jim?

JIM: Dat t'ing, dat make hair grow in yuh hand middle…

GLORIA: *YOU* Jim!

JIM: Yes Gloria.

GLORIA: But Jim …

JIM: A know. All evening A was here an' A couldn't get yuh out
mi mind. A keep looking at yuh picture. A wanted yuh Gloria,
and every turn A turn yuh picture was watching me, so A turn
it round. Gloria, A going say something A never say to you or
admit to miself for twenty years… A love yuh, Gloria.

[*The telephone rings*… JIM *goes into the dining area and
answers it.*]

JIM: Hello… yes… she here.

[*To* GLORIA.]

Overseas for yuh.

GLORIA: Me?

[JIM *throws the phone on the kitchen counter and brushes past her to the bedroom.* GLORIA *picks it up tentatively.*]

Hello? Yes … Who is dat?… Why yuh call me here? Really, for true … Jim!… Hold on… Jim!… Jim! … Jim! Jim, is Paul …

[*He returns.*]

JIM: Paul? Our Paul?

[*She nods.*]

On the phone?

GLORIA: Yes…

JIM: You mad! Hang it up!

GLORIA: He married to a US citizen …

JIM: Paul?

GLORIA: Talk to him.

JIM: Paul – how yuh do? A'm fine. Yuh mother tell me. Is true? For real?

[*He speaks to* GLORIA.]

Gloria, A don't know what to say.

[*He hands her the phone.*]

GLORIA: Talk…

JIM: Dere's a lot A have to say to yuh son, but ahmm … kiss the bride for me an', Paul, take care o' yuhself, an' don't take her for granted. Work together for the good o' the marriage. Take the advice from a experienced married man. Share wid her, listen to what she have to say. Take it seriously, even if she chatting nonsense. Yuh hear what A say … an Paul, make certain the two o' yuh go over the hill together… Is okay. A will explain when A see yuh. Talk to yuh mother…

[*He gives the phone to* GLORIA.]

GLORIA: A will write an tell yuh everything. I love you, too.

> [*She says this to* JIM. *He looks away from her toward the children.*]

Okay mi baby – Bye.

> [*She hangs up. They look at each other.*]

JIM: Jus' you an me alone now …

> [*A knocking is heard at the front gate.* JIM *and* GLORIA *look at each other… then* JIM *looks out through the front door peep-holes.*]

JIM: Is the man who want to buy the house.

> [*Pause*]

GLORIA: Which house? Tell him to go 'bout him business.

> [*She picks up her suitcase and returns to the bedroom. She is by the bedroom window.* JIM *speaks quietly.*]

JIM: We not selling …

> [GLORIA *looks out the window.*]

GLORIA: Jim … Jim!

> [JIM *goes into the bedroom.*]

Jim… the orange tree… it blossoming!

> [JIM *goes toward the window and looks out toward the orange tree.* JIM *is very close to* GLORIA. *She turns away from the window, and their faces almost touch. The closeness makes* JIM *uncomfortable. He backs away.*]

JIM: A will move into Pops's room. A plan to court yuh proper dis time. An' one ting A promise yuh …

> [*He points to the bed.*]

Not before we married.

> [GLORIA *laughs teasingly at* JIM.]

GLORIA: Jim, yuh chatting nonsense. Come here …

> [*She lies on the bed.*]

THE END

School's Out

Performed for the first time at the Barn Theatre, Kingston, Jamaica on 3 April 1975 with the following cast:

RUSS DACRES	Trevor Rhone
MICA MCADAM	Pauline Cowan-Kerr
MR JOSEPHS (JOE)	Vin McKie
HOPAL HENDRY	Vernon Derby
	Teddy Price
PATRICK CAMPBELL	Robert Kerr
REV. STEELE (CHAPLAIN)	Calvin Foster
ROSCO CALLENDER	Oliver Samuels

Directed by Yvonne Jones-Brewster

Characters

RUSS DACRES idealistic, energetic, compassionate; but also pushy, self-righteously eager to assume the role abdicated by the ever-absent headmaster.

HOPAL HENDRY young, unsure, half-educated, ungrammatical, conspicuously under-qualified to teach.

THE CHAPLAIN vain, lecherous, lazy.

MR JOSEPHS (JOE) the most senior member of the staff, he has been at the school for over 20 years. He's an old failure much given to the sardonic, an aging conservative bemoaning the creeping egalitarianism of our times.

ROSCO CALLENDER intelligent, but has taken to playing games.

PAT CAMPBELL an expatriate.

MICA MCADAM young, very attractive, emotionally fickle.

The Language of the characters

MICA, PAT, RUSS, JOE and the CHAPLAIN speak a fairly standard English.

ROSCO uses dialect for effect.

HENDRY attempts to speak the language, but invariably adds an 'h' to words beginning with a vowel, omits it when it is there, and often replaces the 'th' sound with a 'd'.

HENDRY and ROSCO speak dialect much of the time. I have tried to write their speech in such a way that the text may be easily understood by people accustomed to reading Standard English. But the reader or actor is at liberty to articulate in the idiom peculiar to his particular country, provided that the meaning remains intact.

School's Out

The Set   Peeling dirty walls, old books, dog-eared examination papers, defaced maps, piles of rubbish, used milk cartons, empty soft drink bottles with bent-over straws, etc., suggest a cluttered, decaying, dilapidated staff-room.

Up Right an exit leads to classrooms, laboratories, etc. Dominating the set directly Up Centre is a door that leads to the bathroom.

Down Left another exit leads to the car park, the canteen, etc. Down Right, preferably on a lower level, an imposing door reads 'HEADMASTER'. This door is never opened.

Up Left Centre is a small desk with two chairs facing each other on a platform, MR JOSEPHS sits Left. HOPAL HENDRY Right, MR JOSEPHS' old guitar hangs on a nail within his reach.

Down Left above the exit an old broken-down piece of furniture serves as ROSCO's desk. He has no chair.

A long table that seats four dominates Centre Stage running from left to right. THE CHAPLAIN sits Left facing across Right. PAT CAMPBELL sits on his right facing out. Next to PAT CAMPBELL is MICA MCADAM, also facing out. The fourth chair right of MICA will later be taken by RUSS DACRES.

At Stage Right is an old couch. On the wall directly above is the staff room clock.

Up Right in line with the exit is a bookcase with chalk box, attendance registers, etc.

Act One

Scene 1

[*Lights up to reveal the new teacher,* RUSS DACRES, *knocking on the Headmaster's door.* MICA MCADAM *is entering the staff-room from Down Left when she sees* RUSS.]

MICA: Hi. Good morning. [*Very warm and friendly.*]

RUSS: Good morning. I wonder if you could help me.

MICA: I'll try.

RUSS: I am supposed to be joining the staff and I've been trying to find the Headmaster, but he doesn't seem to be in.

MICA: He may be by the general office. It's down to your right, left by the brown building, then … Tell you what, let me take you.

RUSS: Thank you. [*As they are leaving together,* RUSS *is affected by the smell from the overflowing bathroom.*]

MICA: Do excuse the smell. It should have been fixed weeks ago. [*They go out.*]
[*Lights up on* MR JOSEPHS (JOE) *playing his guitar in the staff-room. He too is bothered by the smell. He sprays air freshener towards the bathroom and continues playing his* 'Monday Morning Blues'. HOPAL HENDRY *enters from Up Right and goes directly to his desk.*]

HENDRY: Solicitations on this lovely Monday morning, Mr Josephs. [JOE *pretends not to hear him.*] Mr Josephs!

JOE: Ahm, oh Mr Hendry!

HENDRY: Solicitations on this lovely Monday morning. [JOE *sniffs*.] I see the smell is still smelling strong. [MICA *enters*.] Solicitations to you on this lovely Monday morning, Miss McAdam.

MICA: Yuk!

HENDRY: The smell, eh? One would have thought that after three weeks something would have been done about it.

MICA: Salutations, Mr Josephs.

JOE: [*Laughs*] Good morning, Miss McAdam.

HENDRY: Oh, that is the time? I thought it was later. Never thought I would get here on time, what with all the terrible traffics. The squeeze I squeeze to get on the bus I mashed a lady on her toe who got ignorant and violent and started to trace me, you see?

MICA: My lungs cannot face another week of this stench.

HENDRY: The smell on the bus was worse than the one we have here in this staff-room. Something really has to be done to effect improvement of conditions in school, to facilitate better learning environments for the children and staff alike. Some of the conditions are really shacking. Don't you think so too, Mr Josephs?

JOE: Yes, yes. Shacking! [*Imitating* HENDRY's *speech*.]

MICA: Things have come to a sorry state, haven't they, Mr Josephs?

JOE: Indeed, my dear.

HENDRY: [*Sniffs*] Take my classroom, for example. It is not spacious enough to accommodate the forty-two pairs of desks and chairs, and, even so, some of my students have no place to sit. The cleaners never clean the place. Mind you, I do think most of the children are happier here in this stench than the one they wallow in in their own environments.

JOE: 'But 'tis a common proof that lowliness is young ambition's ladder' etc., etc., etc.

MICA: 'Looks in the clouds, scorning the base degrees.'

HENDRY: That is exactly what I mean. [JOE and MICA *look at each other, not believing his ignorance.*] The rush I rush this morning I leave my tea. I will have to be careful that gas don't take up my stomach. Mind you, with the high gas price, maybe I could open mi own gas station! [*He laughs uproariously at his joke.*] That was a good joke, eh, Mr Josephs? Hilarious! [*No one laughs with him. In fact they are quite stony-faced. HENDRY realises that he is laughing on his own, so he quickly breaks off.*] Let me sign the register. I would hate the headmaster to think I was late.

PAT: [*Entering from Up Right*] Don't any teacher move; this is a smell-up! [*A handkerchief covers his face like a bandit.*]

MICA: Jesus Christ, Pat, it is not funny. I suggest we boycott classes till something is done about it. How do you feel about that, Mr Josephs?

JOE: Let me think about it.

MICA: Mr Hendry?

HENDRY: I too need to organise my mental status, weighing the cons and pros. This matter is, after all…

CHAPLAIN: [*Entering*] Top of the world, fellow members of staff!

MICA: [*Aside to PAT*] Do we have to put up with that on a Monday morning?

HENDRY: Solicitations, Reverend. [*As he pulls out the CHAPLAIN's chair*]

CHAPLAIN: Mr Hendry, good morning. I hope I find everybody well on this lovely Monday morning, fully rested from the vigours of the weekend and raring to go, eh Miss McAdam? Mr Campbell? [*The CHAPLAIN laughs a little dirty laugh at MICA and PAT, who studiedly ignore him.*] I see the smell is no longer with us.

MICA: Jesus Christ!

CHAPLAIN: Mind over matter. Not a thing.

MICA: Yes. Well if the headmaster doesn't do something about it today…

CHAPLAIN: My dear, don't quote me, but it is easier for a camel to go through the eyes of a needle than for one to get the headmaster to lift his little finger to do a single thing to effect the proper running of this school. Don't think I am being uncharitable. As a matter of fact, I know you share my views.

PAT: I am for the boycott, Mica.

CHAPLAIN: [To MICA] My dear, I must say you're looking very charming. Pretty dress, pretty dress. [He touches her.] What's this material? Lovely, lovely! You don't mind do you, Mr Campbell?

MICA: Cheesecloth.

CHAPLAIN: Yes, I do recognise it. I'm a man of the cloth, after all. Cheesecloth, eh? Watch out for mice.

MICA: I hate rats.

ROSCO: [Entering, with a gas-mask over his face, and carrying a small plastic bag with books, etc.] Peace, love, and justice. I come prepared for the smell today.

MICA: From the sublime to the ridiculous.

ROSCO: You like it, Bishop?

CHAPLAIN: It looks good on you. Wear it more often, it improves your image.

ROSCO: Think what it could do for you, Bishop.

CHAPLAIN: Mr Callender, why are always testing my faith? What's this new thing you've taken up, calling me Bishop? I am not flattered. I have no ambitions in that direction.

ROSCO: [Removing gas-mask] Boy, the place smell bad!

MICA: Exactly. We have to make a protest. No classes 'til the smell goes. You with us, Mr Callender?

ROSCO: Sure, but I question if there are not more pressing matters that we should protest about.

CHAPLAIN: Hear, hear!

ROSCO: For example, the question of salaries.

HENDRY: Hear, hear!

MICA: It always comes back to that

ROSCO: The smell don't really bother me. That is minor when you relate it to my total financial distress. Another hundred dollars a month in my pay cheque will make this smell smell like eau de Cologne.

PAT: Come now, Mr Callender, some of us really don't expect to get more money for the amount of work we put in. Some of us are absent more often than we're here.

ROSCO: I know you wouldn't complain or sign a deputation about salaries.

PAT: I can't. I am an expatriate. I'm on contract.

ROSCO: And contracted to get more than me, eh Mr Hendry?

MICA: Naturally, Mr Callender. Pat is a superior teacher, a superior man.

ROSCO: Ah, white is beautiful. Same thing A tell you Mr Hendry. White is beautiful.

CHAPLAIN: Fellow teachers, fellow teachers! [*As he tries to keep the peace.*]

ROSCO: That is the stink we should protest about, Mr Campbell, nothing personal. You don't think so, Bishop?

CHAPLAIN: These are decisions of policy made by the Board and Ministry.

ROSCO: The Board, Bishop? That's the biggest stink of all! Those men don't care about education, Bishop. They climbing the political ladder to glory road – a little pay-off from the party – their own little bit of power. That stink affects the pocket and the intellect. I will sign a deputation to the Prime Minister to get politics out of education. I say get rid of the headmaster. Now, there is an odour! Give me the job, with Bishop as Assistant Head.

CHAPLAIN: Thanks, Mr Callender, but I have no ambitions in that direction either.

ROSCO: Okay, Bishop, you be the Head and I be the assistant.

CHAPLAIN: No thank you, Mr Callender.

ROSCO: You are after bigger stakes, eh Bishop? Like a seat in the senate on the right hand of God.

CHAPLAIN: Mr Callender, you are incorrigible!

ROSCO: Don't forget me, Bishop, when you get into your kingdom. So now, who's going to sign my deputation about salaries? [*The bell goes.* HENDRY *jumps up, picks up register, and is leaving.*] Mark mine for me, or give it to my head boy. [ROSCO *tosses the register at* HENDRY *who catches it and goes out.*]

PAT: [*Searching around on the table*] Where is my blasted register? Why I had to get a form master's job, I don't know. The bloody students hate me and I hate them.

ROSCO: Hey, Joe, you see some test papers about the place? [JOE *shakes his head.*] I have to get out some marks for the headmaster this morning and I just can't find the papers.

PAT: Ah, here it is. Bloody hell! It's not bloody bleeding it. Doesn't this belong to what's his name, Hendry? So it is. 2C. Ten chances to one, he's marking his form with my register. Where do I find 2C?

MICA: Upstairs.

PAT: [*He thinks about it.*] I am not climbing those stairs. [*He relaxes in the couch, hiding* Hendry's *register under the seat.*]

ROSCO: I am tired of how the headmaster hound me for the marks. Where I could put the test papers? I wonder if I leave them down at that girl house.

[*He intrudes on* MICA's *space, and is busy searching among her things. His behaviour is slightly raucous and overbearing, all done deliberately to annoy her. Whether by accident or design, he touches her in a fairly sensitive spot.*]

MICA: Now look here, you! [*In a rage, she is up and out of her chair.*] How the hell did you ever get into a school to teach, like all the rest of you! What am I doing here, in a place like this?

PAT: What you upsetting yourself for, girl?

MICA: But Pat, did you ever see such spineless, vulgar, good for nothing…

PAT: Okay, okay.

MICA: This place gives me the creeps. CREEPS, like bloody stupid Hopal Hendry! Give him time and he'll be the headmaster. And that other slug, can't somebody knot a guitar string around his neck?

PAT: [*who has sat in something rather wet*] Oh no, my, good clean pants!

MICA: Filth! They live in it. Ask them to do something about it and…

PAT: Don't cast your pearls before swine, to quote the almighty vicar.

HENDRY: [*Enters*] I seem to have picked up the wrong register.

PAT: [*Extending his hand for the register*] Thank you. [*He goes and, as* Hendry *starts looking around for 2C's register, the bell goes.*]

CHAPLAIN: Assembly calls. Coming, Miss McAdam?

MICA: I don't believe in God.

CHAPLAIN: [*Looking her up and down in a most lecherous manner*] I would love to save your soul.

MICA: I bet you would. Excuse me. [*Exit* MICA *outside for a breath of fresh air. The* CHAPLAIN *watches her go. His thoughts are very obvious. As she is out of sight, he turns and goes out to the chapel.*]

84

ROSCO: Mr Hendry, help me to look for mi test papers.

HENDRY: I am trying to locate my register.

ROSCO: I will help you look. [*As he sits in the couch, HENDRY searches, while JOE plays his song, getting more and more up-tempo in* JOE's *bad blues fashion. ROSCO watches JOE and appears to be moved by the music.*] Heavy, man. Heavy. You going to record that one? [JOE *shrugs, his body saying* 'Maybe, maybe not'.] That sort of music don't sell. You have to try it with a reggae beat. Titillate the people. [ROSCO *does a reggae beat to which* HENDRY *reacts.*] Look on Hendry, look how it move him.

HENDRY: It nice. [*As he dances.*]

ROSCO: Reggae is a big seller.

[JOE *sniffs, not at the smell, but at* ROSCO's *ideas.*] That is your problem, you are a snob. If you want to make money [*taking the music sheet from* JOE] then all these lyrics will have to change. [ROSCO *reads the lyrics in a very British manner, almost an imitation of* JOE's *speech.*] 'Same old day, going the same old way'. No, no, no, that should be 'Same same day, going di same same way, yeah'. [*He reverts to standard English.*] 'Same old me in the same old bed'. Listen to this version. 'See mi yah, see mi yah in a di same ol' bed, not a ting, not a ting in a mi 'ead'. That's how you have to sing it. [JOE *snatches the music sheet away from* ROSCO.] The School of Music messing up your head, Joe. Black man born to beat drum. [ROSCO *beats out a rhythm on* JOE's *desk.* HENDRY *joins in.*] All them concertos I hear you singing [ROSCO *imitates a fat Italian singer*], no money in that for you. Try it reggae. [JOE, *tired of the interruption, packs his guitar away.*]

JOE: This is a blues. Monday morning blues. It's an expression of my soul. I feel blue.

ROSCO: You feel blue? Boy, you don't look it. To my mind you look wash-out, and if that is the case, then you should call the song 'Monday Morning Wash-out'. If you personally feel blue, don't take it out on the song, take it out on the students. What you think they come here for? I don't understand you, Joe. You have a mental block against the true sounds. Stop writing the tune as a sonata in G for strings. I bet you don't have a single reggae record in your house?

JOE: You have any?

ROSCO: I look like I could afford to buy record?

JOE: Neither can I.

ROSCO: You have 'Back' and 'Choppin'', though. Waste my time talking to you, all the same. Any luck, Mr Hendry?

HENDRY: No, not yet.

[ROSCO *puts the clock back five minutes, and then sees a packet of cigarettes sticking out of* HENDRY's *pocket. With deft fingers* ROSCO *removes the cigarettes.*]

ROSCO: I see you start to buy my brand. [*As he puts a cigarette in his mouth he sticks it out for* HENDRY *to light.* HENDRY *strikes a match and lights the cigarette, but not before* ROSCO *shifts the cigarette around in his mouth, making it as difficult as possible for* HENDRY. *When the cigarette is lit,* ROSCO *blows the smoke in* HENDRY's *face.* ROSCO *pockets the pack, ignoring* HENDRY's *protests.*] Now keep looking for the test papers.

HENDRY: If I had some notion where you might have left them.

ROSCO: How I must know that, Mr Hendry? [ROSCO *finds an old exercise book on the table.*] Hey, look! This exercise book, from Queen Victoria times. Mr Josephs, you better take it.

HENDRY: [*Finding the test papers*] Mister Rosco, is these they?

ROSCO: Them, yes. Cool. Tell you what you do now, help me mark them.

HENDRY: I have to go to assembly.

ROSCO: Forget that, man. Just call out the names for me. Where is mi chair? [*Hiss, as he looks around for it.*] Let me just t'ief the old man's chair, you hear. Where him is? Him gone to assembly or what?

HENDRY: He departed on Friday last.

ROSCO: Him dead?

HENDRY: No, he immigrated to Canada.

ROSCO: To do what? To go dead?

HENDRY: No, he gone to take up a teaching position.

ROSCO: The old man? Joe, is true what Missa Hendry say?

JOE: So it is said.

ROSCO: Him can't do dat. Is not one or two times I sit down here and look across on him and say to myself, 'Rosco boy, is no way you stay here and become like him.' All the time he sit down there quiet-like, him was planning to leave the place. Him must be don't know how Canada cold. They will use him balls to play ice hockey. The man gone and leave me him chair. When Missa Hendry tell me he departed, I was about to push mi hand in mi pocket to contribute towards the wreath. I don't want him chair. I will stand up. Missa Hendry, call out the names and I will work out a mark.

HENDRY: Abrahams, H.

ROSCO: Abrahams. Abrahams. Who is Abrahams? Oh dat boy! Write down fifty. No, dat's too much, make it forty-five. Hold on, when the headmaster see all dem low marks, him will say me not teaching the boys a thing. Make it sixty, you hear, sar.

HENDRY: Brown. Well, I think this one is nought.

ROSCO: Which Brown? White Brown or black Brown?

HENDRY: P. Brown – nought.

ROSCO: How you mean nought?

HENDRY: Di boy didn't do di test, just name and subject.

ROSCO: Oh, is dat Brown! Boy, I have to give him fifty.

HENDRY: But the boy didn't do the test.

ROSCO: Master, is two tyres I lose last month, and I know is that boy Brown responsible. You see the same test here, Joe. Is borrow the boy borrow a pen to write him name, and when I go to collect the test papers, you know what the boy did? Pull out a ratchet knife an' start to clean him finger nails, an' all the while him looking me up an' down. Boy, come to think about it, I wonder if fifty is really enough. Sixty-five look more reasonable.

JOE: You should have reported the boy.

ROSCO: You report him. Don't you have a car too? I don't see a thing on this scene to risk my neck for. Give me them, Mr Hendry. Go to chapel. [*Exit* HENDRY. ROSCO *looks at the test papers.*] This boy is an idiot. Thirty. No, forty. No, thirty. Him is an idiot, even the Headmaster know that. The Headmaster wants marks, and marks he will get. [*He puts the marks down at a furious pace. In the background, the* CHAPLAIN *can be heard preaching.*]

CHAPLAIN: Today's lesson is about the ten virgins. Five were wise and five were foolish, but let me remind the girls of this school that they were all virgins.

ROSCO: Assembly still in progress. Good. One thing about the Chaplain, him can preach. Hey, Joe, I still can't get over how the old man gone. Is three men leave on staff now.

JOE: How you get three?

ROSCO: You, me, Chaplain and Hendry count as one, half each. The expatriate I don't count at all, and the Headmaster... well, the least said, the better. Three men, and the one woman, she look like an adjectival clause, behave like a past participle, but she is really a common noun. [JOE *sniffs.*] Exactly. [*The bell goes.*] What's that?

Assembly over, and I don't finish marking the papers yet. [*He puts the clock forward ten minutes.* MICA *enters to prepare for her class.*] Hey, Joe, what I said about the adjectival clause? Take a good look. [*He laughs.*]

[HENDRY *enters quickly, collects his books, etc. to go off to his class.*]

MICA: Is there any chalk?

ROSCO: My hands are allergic to it, so I don't use it. Where is 4C, Joe?

JOE: I don't teach them.

MICA: Mr Hendry, do you know if there is any chalk?

HENDRY: Look in that box. [HENDRY *is on his way out, as* MICA *looks in the box and screams.* HENDRY *rushes back to the staffroom.*] What happen? What was that noise? [JOE *and* ROSCO *ask 'What happened?'*]

MICA: It's a mouse! [*As she climbs atop the nearest chair.* HENDRY, *hearing it's a mouse, begins to look very uneasy; quietly he sidles away from the bookcase.*]

ROSCO: Where?

MICA: In the box.

ROSCO: [*At the bookcase,* ROSCO *pretends to trap the mouse in the box.*] A little mouse can't do you anything.

[MICA, *seeing* ROSCO *with the box, climbs atop the table.* HENDRY *too is now looking quite scared.*] What's the matter, Mr Hendry, you afraid of him too?

[*As* ROSCO *threatens to throw the box at him.* HENDRY *panics and runs away from* ROSCO.]

HENDRY: No, man, me not afraid of them. [ROSCO *throws the box at* HENDRY.]

ROSCO: See him on the chair leg, Mr Hendry. [HENDRY *joins* MICA *on top of the table.*] See him under the exercise book. [ROSCO *searches among the books on the table for the imaginary mouse.*] Aye, catch it! [*His hands are carefully masked, so* MICA *and* HENDRY *are quite convinced that he's caught it.*] Mr Hendry, a big man like you! [MICA *is getting very hysterical.*]

HENDRY: I just don't like them.

ROSCO: What I must do with it, eh?

MICA: Throw it outside, please. Please.

HENDRY: Yes, yes. Dash it away, man.

ROSCO: You want a bet A just... [*threatens to throw it at* HENDRY.]

HENDRY: Don't do that, man.

ROSCO: What about you, Miss McAdam? [*Edges up to* MICA.]

MICA: I'll kill you! I'll kill you!

ROSCO: All right.

[*As he throws the imaginary mouse at her.* MICA *screams, brushing away the mouse and becoming totally hysterical.*]

HENDRY: Jesus Christ! [*As he leaps from the table onto the couch.*]

PAT: What's going on here?

[RUSS DACRES, *attracted by the screams, runs into the staff room. He stands there transfixed.*]

MICA: I am going to get you! You son of a bitch! [*She pick up a large compass.*]

PAT: Mica!

MICA: Get out of my way, Pat!

PAT: Come, be sensible. Give me the compass. Come on. [*She faints.*] Catch her somebody, quick.

[RUSS DACRES *runs around fast, and along with* JOE, ROSCO *and* PAT, *they catch her in mid-air.*]

PAT: [*To* HENDRY] Get off there. Clear the table. Make some space. [*Just about everything on the table is swept to the floor. Then* MICA *is put down very gently.*] Smelling salts!

ROSCO: Where is the first aid box, Joe?

PAT: I have never seen one.

JOE: There was one here some years ago.

PAT: [To HENDRY] Wet this. [He gives his handkerchief to HENDRY.]

JOE: Here it is. It's empty.

HENDRY: There is no water in the bathroom.

PAT: Brandy, rum, anything!

ROSCO: Yeah, I have a bottle. [Getting it quickly from his desk, he opens it and give it to PAT who wets MICA's face with it. There is no response. RUSS, all this time, is fanning away at MICA.] She coming to?

PAT: No. Get me a glass of water.

ROSCO: Missa Hendry! [HENDRY picks up a glass and dashes out, only to collide with the CHAPLAIN.]

CHAPLAIN: Mr Hendry, what in heaven's name is going on in here?

HENDRY: Is Miss McAdam, Chaplain. She faint away.
[The CHAPLAIN goes quickly to the prostrate MISS MCADAM. The sight is almost too much for him, but he controls himself.]

CHAPLAIN: She needs air. Open all the windows. Let me feel her pulse. Good pulse is there. Heartbeat? [He feels her breast.] Heartbeat is there. Has anybody called a doctor? [To RUSS] Are you a doctor?

RUSS: No. I am the new member of staff.

CHAPLAIN: Get a doctor and I'll say a prayer. Mr Campbell, get on the phone. This is an emergency.

ROSCO: The phone's not working.

CHAPLAIN: Oh Lord, look down from heaven, behold, visit, and relieve this Thy servant. Look upon her with the eyes of Thy mercy.

HENDRY: [Re-entering with the water] The Bishop is coming.

PAT: Christ! Not now. He's never been in here before.

ROSCO: Head him off, Mr Hendry.

CHAPLAIN: Find some excuse.

ROSCO: Just don't let him come in here. Quick!

CHAPLAIN: Spare us the complications, O Lord, and let Mr Hendry be successful in his mission. How is she?

PAT: The same.

CHAPLAIN: There is just one thing else we can try.

PAT: What?

CHAPLAIN: Mouth-to-mouth resuscitation.

PAT: I don't know…

CHAPLAIN: If I can remember my first aid. Pull her blouse. Pull her blouse, man. This is an emergency! Excuse me. [*He pulls her buttons.*] Close your eyes, everybody. If it wasn't an emergency I wouldn't go this far. [*He is awed by her young body. He takes off his collar and sets it on her, then unbuttons his shirt.*] So young. [Slowly his lips descend on hers. She wakes before he kisses her. She slaps him.]

MICA: What the hell! Where am I? Oh my God, what's happening? [*As she discovers her clothes in disarray.*]

CHAPLAIN: It's okay, my dear. We give God thanks. [*The CHAPLAIN rescues his collar from between her legs.*]

MICA: Rape! Rape! [*As she feels his hands on her body.*]

CHAPLAIN: [*Clamps his hands over her mouth.*] Shut up! Aaiee! My finger. The little bit… she bit me.

MICA: Rape! [*As she gets off the table.*]

PAT: Mica, love, it's me – Pat.

MICA: Why didn't you stop him?

CHAPLAIN: Don't be ridiculous. Will somebody explain?

MICA: Where is the Headmaster?

PAT: Don't you remember? You fainted.

MICA: Fainted?

CHAPLAIN: Yes. For one moment I thought you were dead, you were so warm.

MICA: The day you ever try that again, Mr Callender!

ROSCO: Try what again? I was playing a little joke with Mr Hendry. [HENDRY *returns.*] Mr Hendry, I trouble her? [*Shaking his head at him.*]

HENDRY: No. You never trouble her.

ROSCO: I wouldn't be running no joke with you.

CHAPLAIN: Fellow teachers, finish it off. [MICA *goes to the bathroom to freshen up.*] Our new member mustn't get the wrong impression. We haven't met officially. Reverend Steele, with two E's.

RUSS: Russ Dacres.

CHAPLAIN: My pleasure, pleased. I hope your stay here will be rewarding and fruitful. Let me introduce you.

PAT: Patrick Campbell. [Extending his hand.]

CHAPLAIN: One of our stalwarts. Mr Josephs [JOE *does not shake hands with* RUSS, *but holds his hand up in acknowledgement as he goes out.* HENDRY, *who has been picking up the books, etc., from the floor, now positions himself to be introduced.*], our rock of Gibraltar. Been with us for twenty years. [*The* CHAPLAIN *notices* HENDRY's *antics.*] And Mr Hendry, one of our, ahm, promising young educationalists.

HENDRY: I am pleased to make your acquaintance. [*Hanging on to* RUSS's *hand. The* CHAPLAIN *breaks the handshake, and tries to push* HENDRY *into the background.*]

CHAPLAIN: Mr Callender.

ROSCO: [*Dashing off the rest of his marks, looks up but does not stop what he is doing.*] Sorry about the first impression, but I don't dig no black woman who only dig white man [*very loudly*]. It's a personal insult to me, my race, my manhood.

CHAPLAIN: [*As* MICA *enters from bathroom*] Ah, and last but not least, Miss McAdam, our rose among thorns. [MICA *nods to* RUSS, *collects her books and she and* PAT *go out.*]

ROSCO: [*As they leave*] Hypocrite! That girl feel herself superior to every black man in this staff-room.

CHAPLAIN: It's a nice place to work in, really.

ROSCO: She go to some university in North America and feel she is some sort of intellectual. As far as I'm concerned, the only genuine intellectual on this staff is me.

CHAPLAIN: We are a happy family, really.

ROSCO: She don't like me, because I speak so badly. Did you ever hear such asininities? I can use the Queen's English if I so desire, but to me it is no more than an acquisition by the black bourgeois to create barriers and underline the status quo. [*A boy knocks and enters.*] What you want, boy?

BOY: You have us now, sir.

ROSCO: I don't have you now. What form?

BOY: 4C, sir.

ROSCO: Get back to your class. [*The boy hesitates.*] Move, boy!

RUSS: Any idea where I might find the Headmaster?

ROSCO: Boy, I haven't seen him for a month. The man is a hustler. A little politics, a little real estate, a little vegetable garden.

CHAPLAIN: Mr Callender, shame. Ahm, try the canteen. The lady who runs it is very interesting – a divorcee – great favourite with the male members of staff. The Head loves her..er..cooking. Mr Callender never misses a meal. Check the canteen. I'll walk over with you.

[RUSS *looks around for his bag, while the* CHAPLAIN *collects his bible, etc.* ROSCO *gets* HENDRY *quietly into a corner.*]

ROSCO: Hey, not a word to the parson about the mouse.

HENDRY: My lips are seal.

ROSCO: Cool. [*Then sings*]   Hickory dickory dock,
                                       The mouse ran up her frock,
                                       Oh what a shock the mouse
                                       got,
                                       Hickory dickory dock!
[*He and* HENDRY *go off to class.*]

CHAPLAIN: [*As he watches them go*] It's a nice place to work in
    really, apart from the odd gossip, the occasional intrigue,
    the little undercurrents, that sort of thing, plus there is a fair
    amount of backbiting, su-su. Good staff. A few bad eggs,
    naturally, some of them not to be trusted; one or two of
    them, pathetic. And the things I see some of them wearing
    to work! Imagine – no bra! Don't ask me how I know these
    things, but I know. It's not fair…ahm…to the boys.
    Temptation, man, temptation. No wonder there is a
    breakdown of discipline. The Headmaster does his best, but
    he's a little bit insecure, nervous. A political appointment,
    they say. People say all sorts of things about him. Sex maniac,
    interferes with little girls or some such, most uncharitable,
    rumours. He is a good churchman. After you. [*The lights go
    down as they go off.*]

Act One, Scene 2

[*The lights come up on* JOE *in his space and* ROSCO *half-asleep
on the couch.* PAT *and* RUSS *enter the staff-room from Down
Left.*]

PAT: The place is as you see it, the staff as you saw them, a
    bunch of bloody clowns, with one or two exceptions. The
    students, semi-literate mostly. The smell, it grows on you,

conversation piece. Things are bad but we get by. Expect nothing, avoid disappointment. Things won't change, not with jokers around like... Let's not call names, but take a fellow like Callender. He should be banned from the classroom. Does more harm than good. He and the one they call the Chaplain, tongue like a female, mind like a gutter. Money-grubbing capitalistic sex-fiend, bound to go to Heaven.

CHAPLAIN: [*Entering*] Ah, Mr Campbell, I see you are taking good care of our latest addition. You are in good hands. So how is it going, Mr Dacres?

RUSS: Okay.

CHAPLAIN: No trouble with the students?

RUSS: None.

CHAPLAIN: You should have no problems if, like me, you don't spend fifteen minutes to settle your class, like some of the others. You just go in – bang, bang – get some order. If they fool, you run them out. Thirty, if need be. Teach the other five. Many are called, etc, etc. Gospel.

[*The bell goes.* DACRES *collects his things quickly and is on his way out as* MICA *enters. They smile at each other.* PAT *notices, so does* ROSCO.]

ROSCO: Boy, the new man anxious, eh? What a man can move fast! Him will learn all the same. [*He looks directly at* PAT, *smiles mischievously, then picks up a table-tennis bat.* HENDRY *enters as* ROSCO *begins to play with an imaginary ping-pong ball, each shot giving him a great deal of pleasure. Synchronise his smash with the first stroke of the cane offstage.*]

CHAPLAIN: Ah, the Head. [*As he goes over towards the Headmaster's door.*] Whoever is getting it obviously deserves it. A good licking is like a good tonic. [*Whacking continues.*]

Tones up the skin, repels the devils. Never spare the rod. Gospel. Rules are to be obeyed [*whack*]. Each student, boys and girls, should get at least six a week [*whack*]. They thrive on it. Break the law, you'll be punished. Break God's law, you know the consequences [*whack*]. Yes [*whack*]. Yes [*whack*]. Yes. Ahhh! [*Overcome with pleasure.*]

[BLACK OUT]

Act One, Scene 3

[*JOE, HENDRY and PAT are in the staffroom. ROSCO enters from the bathroom.*]

ROSCO: Hey, Joe, inside that bathroom is definitely not right. I will have to start doing my things at my yard. [*Sniff.*] No paper, no soap, no nutten. What they expect a man to use? Plenty old exercise books about, all di same. Only trouble is dat so much crap on them already.
[*The bell goes and HENDRY rises.*]
Where you going?
HENDRY: The bell ring.
ROSCO: I never hear it. Sit down, man. The bell ring, Joe?
JOE: Not to my knowledge.
ROSCO: Sit down, man.
HENDRY: Yes, man, I 'eard it.
ROSCO: Leave me a cigarette. [*Taking HENDRY's pack.*]
[*As HENDRY is leaving the CHAPLAIN comes on from Down Left. RUSS DACRES enters from Up Right with a first-aid kit, books, magazines, etc. MICA follows immediately with a tape recorder.*]

97

RUSS: Ahm, members of staff [*displays first-aid box*], a present for the school.

MICA: And a tape-recorder.

CHAPLAIN: Thoughtful man. Useful thing, eh, Mr Campbell? I have one or two things at home myself. Remind me to bring them in. Is that the time? I must dash. The Prime Minister wants to see me. Ah, Mr Dacres, I should be going to 5B now, but, ahm, could you take charge for me?

RUSS: What shall I do with them?

CHAPLAIN: Just keep them quiet. Thank you. [*Exit CHAPLAIN, RUSS prepares to go but MICA stops him.*]

MICA: The one day he is never away is pay day.

PAT: Mica. [*She does not respond.*]

MICA: Do it once and you're doing it every day.

PAT: Mica! [*Much louder.*]

MICA: Just a second. [*Without looking back at him. PAT is upset by her offhand manner. He leaves the staff room in a huff.*] Don't believe that P.M. rubbish. He's just using that. Self-righteous, power-crazy little bastard!

RUSS: I said I would, so see you at lunch-time [*He goes.*]

MICA: Pat? Where did Mr Campbell go, Mr Josephs?

JOE: Is he in school today? I haven't seen him. [*Exit MICA.*]

ROSCO: [*laughs*] How you mean is the man in school, Joe? Him in school, yes, and it look like him in bad trouble. Yes man, look like Dacres moving in on the white man girl. [*He goes to the tape-recorder and picks it up.*] Nice. I would love a tape-recorder like this. Why Dacres bring it to school? The boys will t'ief it, you know. Him must be don't know di breed o' boys him dealing with. [*He puts the tape-recorder in his bag and away in his desk.*] I think I have a class, but where the hell is mi timetable? I left it here. The Sellotape is still here but the timetable gone. [*Hiss*] Boy Joe, mi head hurting me. I wonder if any Phensic in this thing. [*He picks *up the first-aid kit.*] Hey, Joe, you want a pack? [*Throwing one to him, he pockets two himself.*] What a fat elastic! [*He holds up the rubber band and shows it to* JOE. *Then he starts making a paper shot, at the same time looking around for a fly to fire at. He sees one and quickly makes the rubber band into a sling.*] Watch me and that fly, Joe! [*He pursues it Vietnamese style. Each time he is set to fire, the fly escapes, till eventually it flies through the door.* ROSCO *fires after it, then he panics.*] Jesus Christ, Joe... A shoot the Headmaster!

[BLACK OUT]

Act One, Scene 4

[*Lights up on* ROSCO *and* JOE, *together sharing a form magazine. They read for a moment.*]

ROSCO: Is not a boy write this. No, sir. Nuances licentious, dialectic. [ROSCO *walks away.*]

JOE: I think it's terrible. Apart from that one article which seems very verbose and pompous, the rest of it is sheer dialect nonsense. Better use could be found for the paper.

ROSCO: Not really, Joe. The thing have some merit.
[RUSS *enters the staff-room with a stack of form magazines.*]

RUSS: Mr Callender, you might like to see the first edition of 3A's form magazine.

ROSCO: Thank you, man. [*Accepting a copy.*]

RUSS: Mr Josephs. [*Handing him a copy,* JOE *hands him back the one he was reading.* RUSS *is aware of the snub, yet*

99

presses on]. Ah, Chaplain [*as the* CHAPLAIN *enters*], a copy of 3A's form magazine.

CHAPLAIN: Thank you.

RUSS: Mr Campbell… [*As* PAT *enters. He offers him a copy.*]

PAT: [*Very cuttingly*] I've seen it. [RUSS *puts a magazine in* MICA's *space, then goes up to* HENDRY's *desk. He is putting a magazine down, when an open book catches his eye. He examines it more closely.*]

RUSS: Jesus Christ! [HENDRY *enters and sees him with his book.* RUSS *senses* HENDRY, *and puts the book down.*] Ah, Mr Hendry, I was just leaving you a form magazine. [RUSS *turns away and goes out.* HENDRY *picks up the book, annoyed, looks after* RUSS, *then flicks the magazine off his desk.*]

CHAPLAIN: [*Who has been reading the funnies in the magazine.*] It's a brave effort.

ROSCO: It's all right for a start, but I bet you never see it come out again. Hey, Joe, that Arts magazine you started some years ago, what was the name again? 'Vox'? No, 'Pox', Latin, nuh? Whatever became of it? The boys couldn't dig the classics.

[MICA *enters quickly with a magazine. She is very excited.*]

MICA: Seen the new 3A form magazine, Pat?

[PAT *looks at her, takes the magazine and crumples it very slowly and deliberately, then tosses it away, all the time looking directly at her. The others watch as the lights fade slowly.*]

Act One, Scene 5

[*All members of staff are present, awaiting the Headmaster to have a staff meeting. The* CHAPLAIN *sits in his space,* JOE *has brought his chair down to sit to the left of* PAT. MICA *is in her space beside* RUSS. HENDRY *is Up Stage and* ROSCO *sits atop* JOE's *table.*]

ROSCO: [*Singing in the darkness*] 'Why are we waiting?...Oh why...' [*The lights come up.*] So what time this staff meeting going to start? I don't understand the Headmaster, is the second time him call a staff meeting this term and him don't turn up. Is thirty minutes of my life gone down di drain.

CHAPLAIN: And I have a meeting at 3 o'clock. Prime Minister... [*Mutters.*]

MICA: Waiting here like children. Totally irresponsible.

ROSCO: 'Why are we waiting....' Etc. [*Sings.*]

PAT: He could at least send some message. [*Pause.*]

MICA: Common decency, that's what's lacking, common decency!

HENDRY: I hope he comes, cause there are one or two tings I have to say.

[*A little boy brings in a message.*]

CHAPLAIN: Out! 'Knowest thou that the ground on which thou walkest is hallowed ground?' Out of bounds. Out! [*The boy scampers away followed by the* CHAPLAIN.] What you want? [*The boy hands him the message. He reads it quickly.*] A message from the Head's secretary. The Headmaster regrets that he has been unavoidably delayed and cannot grace us with his presence. [ROSCO *gets off the table and begins to pack away his books, etc. The other members of staff, excluding* MICA *and* RUSS, *also start making a move to leave.*] He further requests that I deputise for him, so I would like to take this opportunity to remind all teachers that they are expected to attend the services on Sunday. There being no further business, meeting dismissed.

ROSCO: Nice.

[*All, except* MICA *and* RUSS, *are on their way out, when* RUSS *stops them.*]

RUSS: Ahm, Reverend Steele, with your permission, there are one or two things I would like to discuss.

CHAPLAIN: With the Head absent, I don't see much point.

[*Again they make to go.*]

RUSS: First thing. This place that we have to work in is a mess. [*Indicates staff-room.*]

MICA: An awful mess.

RUSS: Can anything be done about it?

CHAPLAIN: Well, the Headmaster, you know, hires and fires the cleaning staff. If I was in charge of this place, all the pussy-footing that I see...

ROSCO: What sort of footing, Bishop? [*Much laughter*]

RUSS: Be that as it may, gentlemen, I don't think that any self-respecting teacher can work in a place like this.

MICA: Hear, hear. I've been saying that for months.

HENDRY: Can I express a little view?

CHAPLAIN: Yes. Mr Hendry.

HENDRY: They say that when you throw a stone in a pigsty, the one that bawl is him it hit. But I would like all teachers to cast their eyes over to where I sit. I hope you notice it is meticulous.

RUSS: I'm sorry if I offended you, Mr Henry, but...

HENDRY: Hendry, if you don't mind.

RUSS: No offence meant, Mr Hendry, I am not being personal.

HENDRY: Why are you always picking on me?

RUSS: Mr Hendry?

HENDRY: You 'tink I don't know that you been spying on me, and passing remarks behind my back?

RUSS: Mr Hendry, I don't understand.

102

HENDRY: Excuse me. [*As he grabs his books and makes a very dramatic exit. There is much laughter, making of faces, etc. from* ROSCO, PAT, JOE *and the* CHAPLAIN.]

RUSS: Oh, oh.

CHAPLAIN: I had no idea Mr Hendry was so sensitive.

RUSS: What was that all about? Maybe Mr Hendry's imagination is running away with him. However, what can we do about the staff-room? We are the ones who use the place.

MICA: Why don't we stay one afternoon and tidy it up?

RUSS: That is what I was about to suggest; thank you, Mica.

CHAPLAIN: Uh, yes. Those in favour, say Aye.

[MICA *and* RUSS *raise their hands, and say* 'Aye'.]
Those against?

PAT: Abstain.

ROSCO: Abstain.

CHAPLAIN: Mr Josephs?

JOE: Oh, abstain.

CHAPLAIN: I think it's a matter that has to be left up to each member of staff. Reasonable, Mr Dacres?

RUSS: Reasonable. [*Again they start to leave.*] Just one other thing. [ROSCO *looks at his watch.*] I won't be long. What is the position regarding teachers doing duty at the canteen? I'm not patting myself on the back, but I am the only person here who even bothers to check the duty roster and go to the canteen at lunch or break to try and maintain a little discipline.

ROSCO: But, Missa Dacres, you dealing with hooligans, you must expect hooliganism.

RUSS: That attitude is a reflection of this whole…

ROSCO: Mr Dacres, let me ask you a question. I see you risking your neck in that mess they call a canteen. Things get any better since you start going down there? You achieve anything so far?

103

RUSS: Nothing.

ROSCO: It's a waste of time, right?

RUSS: Right.

ROSCO: Exactly.

RUSS: Exactly what?

ROSCO: Exactly why I never go down there. If you know you going down there to waste your time, why worry?

PAT: I did duty once, and I thought they were serving pork. It wasn't until some time later I realised they were referring to me. Plus one of them picked my wallet that first day. I am never going down there again.

CHAPLAIN: No, no, no! That is not the attitude at all. Members of staff should never neglect their duties.

ROSCO: It's all well and good for you to say that, Bishop, But I never see you down at the canteen yet.

CHAPLAIN: I'm not on the canteen duty roster.

ROSCO: I don't expect to see your name on it. After all, you make up the roster, but at least you could go down there and bless the soul food.

CHAPLAIN: Callender, you are being trivial and irresponsible. I disregard you.

ROSCO: Say what you want, Bishop. I come here to teach. I never come here as a policeman. Let Mr Dacres or the headmaster get two soldiers to man the place, for when that mob storm the raisin-bread counter, is tear gas alone can bring a little order. You people don't know the scene.

RUSS: I know the scene. The reason I can't get anything done down there is simple. No one else bothers to try, so when the boys see me alone down there, how do you think they regard me? As an oppressor. Until everybody on the staff is willing to co-operate, we are going to have this vicious circle. You say the boys are hooligans, and the boys will be hooligans because the staff won't attend duties.

PAT: This is a matter for the Headmaster. [*As he walks out.*]

CHAPLAIN: I think so too, Mr Dacres. This matter falls within his province. [*He goes.*]

ROSCO: Agreed, agreed. [*To* JOE, *sotto voce*] What the man trying to do? To take over the school. [*Loudly*] The Headmaster don't really care, and I follow the leader.

RUSS: That sort of attitude, Mr Callender, is killing this school. What we see wrong is most times what we contribute to, or what we ourselves could in fact stop. But no, we just walk back to the staff room, shrug our shoulders and blame it all on the Headmaster. Most of these things have nothing to do with the Head, but it is a nice way to rationalise away the fact that we are not accomplishing anything.

MICA: I agree with Russ, let us give it a try.

[*The bell goes. Exit* JOE.]

ROSCO: Wait for me, Brother Joe. [*To* MICA *and* RUSS] So that's it for today, folks, and remember if you can't be good, be careful. [*Exit, laughing.*]

PAT: [*Returns angrily*] Coming with me, Mica?

MICA: Yes. [*Exit* PAT, MICA *goes up to* RUSS, *touches him.*] Well, at least we tried. [*She leaves him and rushes out after* PAT. RUSS *is left alone. He looks around at the state of the room. Very determinedly he picks up a number of books and puts them away on the bookshelf, then he stands for a moment surveying the job ahead of him. He throws up his hands in the air despairingly.*]

END OF ACT ONE

Act Two

Scene 1

[*The stage is in darkness. The bell goes. The lights come up. It is lunch-time.* JOE *sits in his space.* MICA *reads a newspaper. Sound effects of* CHAPLAIN *trying to flush the lavatory. Whatever it is that needs flushing, won't.* HENDRY *enters, goes to his desk, puts his books down, and is going out again.*]

JOE: Mr Hendry, going to the canteen?

HENDRY: Yes.

JOE: Two patties and a pint of milk. [*Taking out money.*]

CHAPLAIN: [*Half appearing from bathroom*] A carton of cherry milk. [*Gives* HENDRY *money.*] Bathroom's a nuisance, just won't flush. [*He re-enters bathroom and closes the door as* PAT *enters.*]

PAT: Ah Mr Hendry, an orange juice and a cheese sandwich for me. Want anything, Miss McAdam?

MICA: Orange juice.

PAT: Then it's two orange juices. Now, where is my newspaper? [*Looking directly at* MICA. *She hands it to him. He takes it and sits in the couch.*]

CHAPLAIN: [*Coming from bathroom*] Ah, Mr Campbell, Miss McAdam, what's new? Where is Mr Dacres? [*Chuckles.*] Bathroom's out of order, won't flush. I'd better put up a sign.

[ROSCO *enters as* CHAPLAIN *starts writing the 'out of order' sign.* HENDRY *is just finishing writing the orders in his palm.*]

106

ROSCO: Ah Mr Hendry, the usual: three coco breads, three patties and two pints of chocolate milk, and put it on mi bill, right? [*Exit* ROSCO *to the bathroom.*]

CHAPLAIN: Anybody seen the paste or some tacks?

ROSCO: [*Reappearing from the bathroom, goes to* JOE] Somebody do a thing in that bathroom. I better go and tell Mr Hendry not to bother with the patties. Boy, I have to smoke a cigarette. [*Takes* JOE's *cigarette, pulls on it and gives it back to him.* CHAPLAIN *finds a tack, puts up his sign, goes for his lunch inside his briefcase.*] I am as hungry as hell, but I won't be able to eat those patties when they come.

CHAPLAIN: I would offer you a sandwich, but I know you don't eat pork.

ROSCO: It's against my spiritual religion, Bishop, same way I don't eat lobster, steak or caviar, as it's against my financial religion.

CHAPLAIN: Don't take out your frustrations on me, Mr Callender. If there's something you need that's missing from your life, 'ask and it shall be given unto you'.

ROSCO: Who I must ask, Bishop?

CHAPLAIN: God!

ROSCO: Oh, well, him don't like my face, or the way I talk, 'cause him never pay me any attention.

CHAPLAIN: Maybe because, like me, your faith is not strong enough.

ROSCO: Bishop, you're the luckiest man I know.

CHAPLAIN: It's not luck. I heard the word of God and I sought out God and that's how I got my faith.

ROSCO: Sounds reasonable, Bishop; but, Bishop, I don't know where to look.

CHAPLAIN: Didn't you hear about God when you were a little boy?

ROSCO: Sure, and I heard about Hitler, Mohammed, Mussolini.

CHAPLAIN: Mr Callender, I will pray for you.

ROSCO: No, thank you, sir. If your God is the type of God who would dismiss me so, then I prefer to go to hell.

CHAPLAIN: God is a good God, Mr Callender. Think of the rain, the flowers, the food we eat. Thank God for these things.

ROSCO: You don't thank God for the hurricane and the earthquake, I am not thanking him for the sunshine. I don't understand you, Bishop. Last drought you prayed for rain, then a storm threatened, and you prayed for it to pass.

CHAPLAIN: And it did pass.

ROSCO: Sure it pass.

CHAPLAIN: The power of prayer, Mr Callender.

ROSCO: It pass here, but it smash into Cuba, and you go back to the church and thank God for His mercy. So what happen to the Cubans, Bishop? Don't tell me is because them is communist, and them wicked, I hear that argument from you already. You only pray for yourself. Tut, tut, tut, selfish, Bishop.

CHAPLAIN: The devil comes in many guises, Mr Callender, to test my faith, but I will pray for you in the hope that one day you will be able to do something worthwhile with your life, for now you are in the throes of darkness.

[*He looks around to see that* ROSCO *is now wearing a paper collar.*]

ROSCO: Hey, Joe, heard thou ever of the parable of a young lass who visited a certain physician, and complained thereof of an indisposition? And it came to pass that he [*pointing to the* CHAPLAIN] examined her and found that she was with child. Whereupon, the young virgin [*he bows to* MICA, PAT *sniggers*], for so she termed herself, was much alarmed, and cried, 'impossible, for as yet I have known no man'. Hearing these words, the physician opened a window and gazed into the heavens, and many hours did he spend there-a-gazing. And the young lass, on seeing this, was puzzled, and inquired of him, 'Why dost thou so gaze into the heavens?' And he replied, 'My good woman, the last time this phenomenon happened, a star rose in the East, and I am not going to miss it this time' [ROSCO *and* PAT *laugh uproariously.* MICA *chuckles. Even* JOE *manages a smile. The* CHAPLAIN *is stony-faced.*] And there is another one about a Bishop.

CHAPLAIN: We've heard that one before, Mr Callender.

PAT: I haven't.

CHAPLAIN: Don't encourage him, Mr Campbell. [HENDRY *enters empty-handed.*] So Mr Hendry, where is the lunch?

HENDRY: No lunch.

ROSCO: What you mean, no lunch? The canteen staff on strike again?

HENDRY: Is not a strike. Mr Dacres take it upon himself to lock down the canteen.

ROSCO: Lock it down! What you mean?

HENDRY: It was the usual situation where the students storm the place; so Mr Dacres say, if no line, no lunch. [*Non-verbal reaction from the rest of the staff.* JOE *stops playing; the* CHAPLAIN *stops chewing:* PAT *looks up from his paper;* MICA *listens keenly.*] They ignore him, so him lock the door, and is then the riot start. One boy broked a bottle and start to threaten Mr Dacres. [*Exit* MICA *quickly towards the canteen.*]

CHAPLAIN: This situation is becoming very interesting, eh Mr Campbell?

ROSCO: But line don't apply to you, Mr Hendry?

HENDRY: As a member of staff, I thought I had certain privileges so I bored my way through the students and positioned myself at the door. Mr Dacres tell me sorry, he can't let me in, so I explain to him that I am a member of staff and I have certain privileges. Him say him don't business with that – 'no line, no lunch.' What I must do is get the students to form a line. I wasn't staying down there. You should hear the indecent language. The more Mr Dacres defend the door, the more they storm it, the more him push them. Him t'umped a boy in him mouth, blood gash. Is like a riot, I tell you. I have never seen such violence.

PAT: [*Interpolating throughout the brief exclamations*] And where is the Headmaster in all this?

HENDRY: He is off the premises.

PAT: So who is running the school? Is it Mr Dacres? Is he the new Head? I'd love somebody to tell me. Close the canteen? Can any member of staff, a junior at that, take it upon himself to take this sort of unilateral decision? God knows I'm hungry, but it's more than that, there are principles involved. The man walks in, takes over, what gives him the right? I don't know about you people, but I am not going to sit back here and allow this situation to continue. I am not going back to class until I get something to eat. I am prepared to sit here all day and all next week if needs be, and if the Head wants to know why I haven't been to class, I will tell him.

[MICA *enters with orange juice and sandwich for* PAT, *cherry milk for the* CHAPLAIN, *and juice for herself. She waits on them.* PAT *ignores food and* MICA.]

MICA: There is a line now. Everything is orderly.

PAT: What's this thing about him punching a boy in his mouth and there's blood all over the place?

MICA: Blood? Oh, he pushed a boy or two, but no blood. Oh Mr Hendry, there is a message for you from Mr Dacres. He says you may now come for your lunch.

110

HENDRY: I am not hungry. [*Very angrily*]

ROSCO: I hungry bad. [*He points* HENDRY *towards the canteen.*] Put it on mi bill, don't forget. [HENDRY *is on his way when the bell rings. He stops and returns to his desk.*] What happen?

HENDRY: The bell ring.

ROSCO: I never hear it, man.

HENDRY: I have a class. [*Collects his books and goes out in the direction away from the canteen.* PAT *follows him immediately.*]

ROSCO: Is a good thing I'm not hungry. I better check if I have a class. [*He does.*] I have a class, yes, I going to eat. [*Exit towards the canteen, meeting* RUSS *on the way.*] Hail the man!

[CHAPLAIN *pats* RUSS *on his back.*]

CHAPLAIN: Keep up the good work. [*As he goes out.* JOE *too goes out.*]

MICA: [*To* RUSS] I never thought it was possible. Nice.

RUSS: Somebody had to do something. [*They look around the staff-room and decide to have a go at tidying up.* PAT *and* HENDRY *come on, on the lower level.*]

PAT: What's the name of the boy he punched in the mouth?

HENDRY: Ahm, I don't remember his name.

PAT: You could recognise the boy, though?

HENDRY: There was so much confusion that it would be difficult.

PAT: Let him keep it up.

HENDRY: Somebody is going to fix him business. Insult me in front of the students! Some of the rumours I hear about him and some of the girls in this school!

PAT: Rumours, Mr Hendry? What rumours?

HENDRY: I am a man that mind mi own business, so I have nutten to say. But make him fool wid me. I can be a real

Mother Long-Tongue. Mi temper short and I can spread rumours.

PAT: Well, Mr Hendry, maybe I shouldn't tell you this, but he's been saying that you are not qualified for this job. [*Pause, as he lets it sink in, noting the effect on* HENDRY.] The Headmaster should know what's going on in this school. Someone should say something to him, and you may be the best person to do it. He thinks a lot of you, I know that. Only the other day I heard him say that you were his right-hand man.

HENDRY: He really said that?

PAT: That's what he said.

HENDRY: Huh! [PAT *guides him over to the Headmaster's door.* HENDRY, *slightly unsure of himself, knocks tentatively.* PAT *offers encouragement from a distance.* MICA *and* RUSS *continue to tidy the staff-room as the lights go down on the scene.*]

Act Two, Scene 2

[*Lights up on a reasonably tidy staff-room.* ROSCO *enters, and is surprised at the transformation. A look of real mischief crosses his face as he decides to put the place back to how it was before.* ROSCO *sets to work tossing books, paper, etc. in the air and letting them fall where they will. Among the papers he finds a comic. His face lights up with pleasure, but he needs time to read it. The* CHAPLAIN *enters and catches him putting the clock back. Moments later* JOE *comes on.*]

CHAPLAIN: Have you just finished a class, Mr Josephs?
JOE: Yes.

CHAPLAIN: So the bell has gone.

JOE: I don't go by the bell.

CHAPLAIN: Some days it's fast, some days it's slow. I don't understand it. [*Exit.*]

ROSCO: Hey, Joe, give me a hand with this table.

JOE: You joining the Crusader's tidy-up campaign?

ROSCO: What you call him? Crusader! Is a nice name. Joining him? No, man. As Mr Crusader tidy, so I untidy. Is war. The man should be at public cleansing. The place don't feel right tidy, Joe – uncomfortable. Ashtray and all – nice. [*He picks up the ashtray and examines it.*] Boy, this would look good on my bedside table. [*Put ashtray in his bag.*] Good old Chinese proverb, you know, Joe, 'Ash on floor keep tray clean'. [*Then he gets another thought.*] Hey, Joe, pass me that ruler.

[ROSCO *picks up another ruler and puts them together in the shape of a cross. He uses the masking tape to affix it to* RUSS's *space.*] If the man was fighting for more salary I would support him, but what him hope to get out of all the things him doing in the school? No promotion in this job, unless is the Headmastership him after. Then him really have no ambition. [*The* CHAPLAIN *enters to look at the time.*] Man get to school before day break, leave after dark. Those little girls in third form will rape him, you know. Him better watch himself that them don't start spread some serious rumours 'bout him.

[RUSS, *on his way to the Head's office with* HENDRY's *reports, meets the* CHAPLAIN *on the way out of the staff room.*]

RUSS: Ah, Chaplain, I am starting a welfare organisation in the school for the underprivileged children.

CHAPLAIN: Absolutely splendid idea! It's been knocking around my head for months.

RUSS: About how us organising it together?

CHAPLAIN: Love to, but, ahm... Let me check my commitments for the rest of this term...ahm...this term is bad. Pressures of school and church, plus I am on one of the Prime Minister's committees. How about next term?

RUSS: I'd like to start right away.

CHAPLAIN: This term is definitely out for me. [*The bell goes.*] After you. [RUSS *goes to the Head's office.* CHAPLAIN *returns to the staff-room.*]

ROSCO: I have a class, but where are the books?

[JOE *goes to the bathroom.* ROSCO *puts the clock forward ten minutes and sits in the couch.* PAT *and* MICA *arrive.*]

PAT: Something must be wrong with the clock. That was the longest forty minutes.

CHAPLAIN: Something is definitely wrong. Now it's running fast.

MICA: It's no use reporting it to the Head.

PAT: I don't suppose Mr Dacres knows about it, eh Miss McAdam? [*Sarcastically.*]

CHAPLAIN: Good man, that Mr Dacres, good man. Now where do I go next, Heaven or Hell?

RUSS: [*Entering*] Any one seen Mr Hendry?

MICA: I think he's teaching.

RUSS: Have you seen his comments on these reports? [*Show them to her.*] That is ridiculous. The Head cannot send these to parents. Did you see these, Mr Josephs?

JOE: Yes, but I noticed nothing unusual. [MICA *laughs.*]

RUSS: Listen to this one. Davis – 2C History – 'He his making good progress.' H – I – S!

JOE: That is not unusual for Mr Hendry.

RUSS: What about this one. King – 2C – 'He as not learn his lesson.' These can't go out. How long has this man been teaching here?

MICA: Too long.

RUSS: And the Head?

PAT: 'E his 'is favourite teacher. What can 'e does?

[*Everyone laughs except* JOE *and* RUSS.]

RUSS: And you? [*To* PAT]

MICA: What can we do, Russ? The Head sees it, knows it, does nothing.

PAT: The Head's a sensitive man, Mr Dacres. I wouldn't want him to think I was taking over his job.

CHAPLAIN: Leave well alone is what I say.

RUSS: But this man is creating havoc in the school.

CHAPLAIN: A move against Hendry is a move against the Head, who whether we like it or not, is the constituted authority.

[HENDRY *enters.*]

RUSS: Ah, Mr Hendry?

HENDRY: What is it?

RUSS: Have a look at this. Does it make sense to you?

HENDRY: What?

RUSS: This report.

HENDRY: What about it?

RUSS: Read.

HENDRY: What's wrong? I don't see anything wrong.

RUSS: 'He his'? H – I – S! 'He as not learn'?

HENDRY: Oh that, just a little slip of the pen. [*He attempts to correct it. Titters from the rest.*]

RUSS: A little slip, Mr Hendry? You slip on every report. As a teacher with some sort of responsibility to the students, I am going to take it upon myself to tell you that these reports will have to be done all over again. Here you are, sir. [*There is a long pause until* HENDRY, *red in the face, turns and walks out of the room, leaving* RUSS *with the reports.*] How could that fellow get in to teach?

JOE: The day he walked into this staff-room, I saw it as the beginning of the end.

[PAT *leaves in search of* HENDRY.]

CHAPLAIN: The man has done more harm than good. Mr Dacres, let me be the first to congratulate you. A few more people with your guts and determination on this staff, and things would really get moving. You have given me hope for the future. I am telling you before your face because I cannot play the hypocrite. [ROSCO *laughs and goes out.*] You are doing some excellent work. We are behind you. We have to join hands with Mr Dacres, don't you agree, Mr Josephs?

JOE: Isn't it too late?

CHAPLAIN: That's a very defeatist attitude, Mr Josephs.

JOE: No. Years ago, I used to try this, and try that. I too had dreams of a new Jerusalem. Look what I end up with, a desk next to Hopal Hendry.

CHAPLAIN: Hendry should go.

JOE: [*Stands and comes down to the* CHAPLAIN *who is the right of* RUSS.] I agree in principle, but what happens when we get rid of Hendry, who do we get instead? [*To* RUSS] There's a never-ending steam of Hendrys yet to come. Yet I don't blame the man. It's not his fault he is here. We have to see him in terms of the breakdown of the social order and the dilemma in education, brought about by the concepts of the new social mobility.

CHAPLAIN: Words, words.

JOE: So when you attack Hendry [*pointing to* HENDRY's *chair*], you attack a greater dilemma. He is no isolated case. The man is a symbol of the decadence and decay that has come upon us since Independence. Fourteen years ago there would have been no place for Hendry in this school. Not as a teacher, not as student. It would have been unthinkable. He would be totally unacceptable. This school had a reputation and a tradition.

RUSS: A little corner for the elite and a few lucky blacks with pretension – that's all it was, Mr Josephs.

JOE: At least we had standards! What have you put in its place? The rabble I have to be teaching [*pointing to* HENDRY's *chair*], and some of the rabble I see teaching! People like you cry down the past, but if what I see happening around me today is any reflection of the future, then I say, 'Up the good old days'! Folks knew who they were, Mr Dacres; they knew their place, they were happier for it. Now the Philistines are in control. Listen to the modern-day garbage on the radio. Hopal Hendry to me is what reggae music is to Bach. Standards had to fall. Everything of value's been rejected. The English language is a perfect example.

RUSS: There is something to be said for the dialect, it's the language of the people.

JOE: I don't agree. This is an English-speaking country. Everything should be done to get the children to appreciate the English language. If Shakespeare is best in the language, then we continue with him. If Latin helps, then we do Latin.

RUSS: Nonsense. The dialect is more valid than Shakespeare.

JOE: This is not a pantomime, a cheap vaudeville show designed to titillate the vulgar appetites of the masses.

RUSS: The dialect is valid communication. As a teaching language, it should be encouraged.

JOE: You don't really mean that?

RUSS: I do. The curriculum has to be geared to the needs of the people. What does the country need to survive? French or agriculture? The time spent propping up the Eiffel Tower should be spent teaching agriculture.

JOE: You know, Mr Dacres, it's people like you who must take responsibility for people like Hendry. You are a contradiction. You go around the school shouting, 'Up with the people, help the sufferers, go down to the masses!' And when the masses get into power, you wonder how they ever got up there, and want to get rid of them. After twenty years, how do you think I feel to see things come to this? In a way, though, I know good sense will prevail. If not, we will be lost forever in the jungle of ignorance and vulgarity. Pray God I will not be around to see it happen! Excuse me! [JOE *strides out of the room.*]

CHAPLAIN: Well, well, well.

MICA: Somebody over-reacted. That man is totally against any sort of change. All he ever talks about are the good old days. Bloody colonialist!

CHAPLAIN: I think Mr Josephs goes back much further than colonialism. I see him as an Old Testament character.

MICA: The trouble with Mr Josephs is that he's caught between two worlds and living in none.

CHAPLAIN: And he's a snob, totally arrogant. He teaches his French with total disdain. I've heard him say that he has no intention of casting his pearls before swine. Mr Dacres… [*He extends his hand to* RUSS, *who ignores him as the bell goes.*]

MICA: Oh, I have a class.

RUSS: May I walk down with you, Mica?

MICA: Yes, please. [*They go out, leaving the* CHAPLAIN *with his hand still extended. He withdraws it, then goes out.*] [HENDRY, *really furious, comes storming into the staff-room.* JOE *follows.*]

JOE: I know how you feel. The man embarrassed you, but relax.

HENDRY: Relax, Mr Josephs? Not the way I feel. Ooh! [*As he boils.*] If him all come in here now, I would take something an' lick him down. I will kick him an' go to court house an' pay for it.

JOE: That won't be necessary. See the man for what he is, a trouble-maker. There are people like him all over the place. Relax yourself. He is not the Headmaster here.

HENDRY: I come here before him, an' him going to leave me here.

JOE Now you making sense.

HENDRY: I am going to tell him that, and I plan to talk loud when I talking, because I want him to hear. Who him think him is? God's gift to education? What him think that is him one know everything? I don't come here under false pretences. I come as a train' teacher. I fulfil all the requirements for this job. I come here highly recommended. I have a piece of paper at my yard that I can show. I arrive at the top of my class. All at college, is all B plus and A minus I use to get. And the Headmaster don't have no complaints about me so far, an' is eighteen months since me is here. If him had faults to find, him would find it already. If anybody work in this school, is me.

JOE: I know, I know. I had to defend you.

HENDRY: I am never absent. I am never late. My marks is always in on time.

JOE: I know. I came to your defence.

HENDRY: So if that Mr Dacres think that I am going to stand back an' let him snatch bread out mi mouth, then is going to be war in here. I work hard to reach where I reach, and nobody going to push me around. Before that, I draw blood. Is liberty or death. Is a free country and I don't want no boss to slave-drive me. [*Enter* ROSCO.]

ROSCO: What's happening, fellers? Mr Hendry, how you head looking so square?

HENDRY: Mr Rosco, this is no time for jokes. Serious things going on.

ROSCO: Like what?

JOE: Crusader is over-stepping his mark, man.

ROSCO: I tell you already how to deal with that feller. Ignore him. Him soon burn himself out. What him really want is a girl. That man have too much energy.

HENDRY: From what I hear, him have a girl.

ROSCO: Who? McAdam?

HENDRY: No, a girl in 5B, the one with the big bosom. The one they call 'Hamper'. I think Wilhelmina Hermit is her real name.

ROSCO: Rumours, man.

HENDRY: Is so I hear. [ROSCO *sees* RUSS DACRES *approaching. He signals to* HENDRY.]

RUSS: Mr Callender.

ROSCO: What's happening, Mr Dacres? Sit down, nuh?

RUSS: [*Still standing*] You have any idea who should be teaching 4F at this moment?

ROSCO: 4F, 4F? We have a 4F? I don't think we have a 4F, you know, Mr Dacres.

RUSS: There is a 4F, Mr Callender. Next door to 4E where I was teaching a minute ago.

ROSCO: Brother Joe, any idea where the master timetable is? I don't believe there is a 4F at all. This man say so, but I don't think so.

RUSS: Yes, Mr Callender, and if I'm not mistaken, you should be with them now.

ROSCO: Me? No, sir.

RUSS: Yes sir. The class you walked out of a few minutes ago. That's 4F! Well, they're running riot all over the corridor.

ROSCO: Is 4F? I never know that. This school is too big.

RUSS: Anyway, I can't get a word in to my class, because of the noise from next door. I wonder if you could do something about it?

120

ROSCO: I am not going back up there until they learn to behave themselves. You know what a boy did to me up there, Joe? Mr Hendry, listen to this. A run the boy, what him name, out of the class. Boy give me a whole heap o' trouble. Boy tell me say him not leaving, so A grab him an' push him outside. [*Acts it out with* DACRES.] The boy come back and start to make up a whole heap of noise 'bout freedom, justice, socialism, human rights, education code, United Nations Charter and process of participation, so A run him again. Boy hiss him teeth and wouldn't move, so me walk out. Until him apologise, I not going up there again.

RUSS: That's not the attitude.

ROSCO: Eh? [*Surprised.*]

RUSS: I teach those boys and I have no problems with them.

ROSCO: Well, master, you welcome to them.

RUSS: Running the boy out of the class doesn't solve the problem.

ROSCO: Mr Hendry, you have a cigarette? [HENDRY *is smoking.*]

HENDRY: Just this.

ROSCO: Give it to me then, nuh? [ROSCO *takes it.*]

RUSS: Your attitude is not helping to solve the problems of discipline in this school.

ROSCO: Discipline! [*Hiss.*] You see all the boy mi run out the class, is only one way to deal with that sort of discipline problem. I wish they would make me Headmaster, I know exactly what I would do. I would construct a Gun Court in the middle of the play field; and come Monday morning, right after Chapel, I would make the whole school gather right round the wire fence, then I would catch the boy and let the parson administer the last rites. Then I would tie up the boy and call the cadets with the long guns and

121

– bang, bang, bang! Then you would see a little discipline in this school. Boy, I wish they would make me Headmaster!

RUSS: In the meantime, what are you going to do about 4F?

ROSCO: What you say? What am I going to do about 4F? There is nothing I can do about 4F until they make me Headmaster; nothing anybody can do. You know what the 'F' stand for? I don't understand you all the same, you know, Mr Dacres. You leave from upstairs to come down here to worry about my 4F. I bet all now your 4E running riot too. You really not serving any purpose down here. I am not going back; and, by the look of things, you not going back either, so the two of us can stay here and rap. Mr Hendry, any more cigarettes?

HENDRY: That was the last one.

ROSCO: Go buy some, and pass the race form for me; look in mi desk. And on your way out pass by 4F and see what going on.

RUSS: Are you going back to 4F or not? I would like to continue my class.

ROSCO: In a minute.

RUSS: Why you boys keep up with this rass attitude all the time? I just cannot take it, man.

ROSCO: Hold down, man. This is a church school. Suppose the Bishop was to walk in here.

RUSS: As a pin drop, you walk out the class. You don't give a damn for the students.

ROSCO: [To HENDRY] This is last week's race form, man. Pick up a new one. Pass that for me all the same.

RUSS: You have no conscience.

ROSCO: Why you going on like that? Mind you get a heart attack.

RUSS: Mr Callender!

ROSCO: Rosco, man. Bruck down the formalities.

RUSS: Mr Callender, about 4F?

ROSCO: Change the subject, nuh, man? What a man persistent!

RUSS: If you had any conscience, you would resign.

ROSCO: Finish the argument, nuh, man? Is a good thing me nuh married to you!

RUSS: Why don't you have a little response…[*The bell goes.*]

ROSCO: [*Smiles*] Saved by the bell.

[BLACK OUT]

Act Two, Scene 3

[*The lights come up on* PAT *and the* CHAPLAIN *talking together in the staff-room.*]

CHAPLAIN: I am totally upset, Mr Campbell. The man didn't even as a 'by your leave' extend me the courtesy. Next things I hear is that a Welfare Society is started in the school, right under my nose, and after all, welfare is *my* type of work. People are my business; all my life, the welfare of people has been my concern. The man didn't even have the common decency to consult me.

PAT: He said he did ask you, but you didn't have the time.

CHAPLAIN: Not a word to me. I would have found the time. People are my business. He's making me out to be a liar. The man is trying to undermine my position and authority. Parents have been approaching me, wanting to know how it's going. I don't know what to say. I feel like a fool. Why is the man trying to embarrass me?

[RUSS *enters.*]

123

RUSS: Hello, sir. Mr. Campbell.

[PAT *acknowledges him non-verbally. The* CHAPLAIN *beams and is most charming.*]

CHAPLAIN: Top of the world to you! [RUSS *collects a book and leaves.*] He didn't hear me. [PAT *shakes his head.*] Same thing with the Chapel. Worship is compulsory. It's a rule for the school. On Wednesday last, five boys from that Rastafarian element absented themselves from service, so I sought them out. All were from Dacres' class. Naturally I challenged him about it. Do you know what the man said? That he wonders whether a boy brought up in the Rastafarian tradition should be forced to attend a Church of England service. So I explained to him that Chapel is compulsory. Chapel is compulsory.

PAT: My main quarrel with the man, apart from his trying to destroy the Christian principles of the school and his general hanky-panky with fellow members of staff, is that the man is a racist, always giving off those black sounds.

CHAPLAIN: An attitude that is totally unnecessary and against the Christian principle of 'love thy neighbour', and totally against our national motto and the immortal words of our beloved Prime Minister – 'The word is love'. [*Enter* JOE.] Have you heard the latest, Joe? Mr Campbell has been under attack on the grounds of colour, from guess who? [*Sticking his chin out towards* RUSS's *chair.*]

JOE: The man is a trouble-maker. Yes, I have heard him question your involvement.

PAT: My involvement?

JOE: You being an outsider.

PAT: I've been on this staff for two years, you are the people most able to judge. Haven't I been pulling my weight, contributing to the welfare of this country?

JOE: Pat, I've been on this staff for twenty years. In that time I've seen the Dacres of this world come and go, like footprints on the beach, the impression is temporary.

CHAPLAIN: Well said, eloquently expressed! [*Applauds.*] Dacres will burn himself out.

PAT: He is interfering more every day, if you ask me.

JOE: Dying embers always burn brightest before they fade.

CHAPLAIN: This man should have been a poet. Let me write that down. I must fit it into Sunday's sermon. 'Dying embers always burn brightest before they fade.'

PAT: Nonetheless, I think a report of his activities should be made to the Headmaster.

CHAPLAIN: No, man, heed the words of prophecy from the lips of Mr Josephs, poet, artist, linguist, musician, a man who has dedicated twenty years of his life to the cultural growth and expansion of young minds. The flash-in-the-pan miracle worker will burn himself out.

PAT: You know who has really suffered? Poor Mr Hendry, Hopal. Dacres sits on him daily. It's a bloody shame!

CHAPLAIN: Not a bad fellow, you know. Hopal tries hard, he's conscientious.

JOE: Right now he is on the verge of a nervous breakdown.

PAT: Dacres has completely undermined his confidence.

JOE: He has developed this nervous twitch. Have you seen it? [JOE *twitches.*]

CHAPLAIN: Poor fellow.

JOE: The students have picked it up now. All over the school you can see them. [*He twitches again.*]

CHAPLAIN: Poor boy needs a bit of sympathy. [*Enter* HENDRY.] Ah, Mr Hendry, we were just talking about you and that fly-by-night Dacres. We were saying that in the face of great adversity you have behaved like a true gentleman.

HENDRY: [*Twitches, and all his books fall to the floor.*]

I tell you, my cup runneth over. My emotions are hard to be contained.

PAT: Mr Hendry, don't ever let him upset you. [*As he helps to pick up* HENDRY's *books.*]

CHAPLAIN: We are behind you my friend, totally. We know and appreciate your worth. [*As they seat* HENDRY *in the* CHAPLAIN's *chair.*]

JOE: That's what I have been telling him.

CHAPLAIN: We will have to stick together against that wicked man, a troublemaker with deep psychological problems. Long after he is gone you will still be with us.

HENDRY: Over the last number of months I have undergone a terrible strain. [*Twitches.*]

CHAPLAIN: Shame!

HENDRY: I go to bed at night and I wake up in the morning and my head does not touch the pillow, for I don't sleep a wink. [*Twitches.*]

PAT: Shame!

HENDRY: Trials and tribulations I know are in this world; but what I have done to deserve this, I don't know.

CHAPLAIN: Chin up, man, chin up.

HENDRY: It is heart-warming to know that some people on the staff, at least, are appreciative of my services.

CHAPLAIN: We are indeed.

PAT: And don't forget the Headmaster who loves you.

HENDRY: Yes, he is aware of the many things that has been tried by me to inoculate discipline and a sense of purpose into the children whose responsibility rests in my hands.

CHAPLAIN: And we love you too, as a friend and a brother. Don't we, gentlemen? Keep the faith and put your trust in Jesus.

[RUSS *is seen at the entrance. The group breaks up.* ROSCO *calls out to* RUSS. *They talk at the Down Left entrance to the staff-room.*]

ROSCO: Hey, Mr Dacres! Is none of my business, right, but some serious rumours going around the school. I think you should try and put a stop to them.

RUSS: Mr Callender, they are what they are, you know – rumours.

ROSCO: But I...

RUSS: Anyway, thanks for bringing it to my attention.

[*He continues to the staff-room. ROSCO looks at him, then exit to the outside. Exeunt the CHAPLAIN, JOE, HENDRY and RUSS to class. PAT and MICA remain.*]

PAT: Miss McAdam. Mica. I must talk with you, as a friend.

MICA: Yes?

PAT: What's going on between Dacres and that girl in the fifth?

MICA: What girl?

PAT: The rumour is all over the school. What's her name? Wilhelmina Hermit? The way I heard it, she is your rival.

MICA: Augh!

PAT: You must have heard something. Snigger, snigger, snigger. One day its Miss McAdam and Mr Dacres are doing a thing. Now it's Wilhelmina Hermit take away Miss McAdam's man. They have been seen together, in and out of school. I don't say hanky panky is going on, but it does look odd. It's not fair, involving you in this sort of scandal.

MICA: I don't believe it.

PAT: Somehow you have to squash these rumours. The things being said about you are most uncomplimentary.

MICA: Mr Campbell, I am an intelligent woman. The intelligent thing to do is to ignore it.

PAT: Maybe, but this thing with her is, I gather, really a passionate love affair.

CHAPLAIN: [*Entering*] Love affair? Who's having a love affair? Tell me about it. I bet it's not as interesting as what I just overheard from a couple of students.

MICA: I would ignore it.

CHAPLAIN: Naturally I dismissed it as rumour. I had to. One doesn't expect this sort of thing to happen in a respectable Church school, particularly when a supposedly respectable member of staff is involved, particularly one that goes on like he is the new Messiah.

PAT: Exactly.

MICA: Excuse me. [*Exit.*]

CHAPLAIN: She'll discover the truth. That man Dacres is a snake in the grass.

PAT: Carrying on with a schoolgirl is one thing, but...

CHAPLAIN: Schoolgirl? What schoolgirl?

PAT: Wilhelmina Hermit.

CHAPLAIN: That wasn't what I heard. Hermit? No. It wasn't with a girl, it was with one of the boys.

PAT: What! One of the boys?

CHAPLAIN: So it's been rumoured. You know the boy, half-Chinese fellow, name's Lowe. Lowe in name, low in nature, low in stature. Feminine, wears sandals. I've always been suspicious of him.

PAT: Now you say it, certain things do come back. So what about this thing with him and the girl?

CHAPLAIN: It's very likely that he could be... ahm... ambidextrous.

PAT: It's not impossible.

CHAPLAIN: Wouldn't put anything past him. Something very strange about that man. He and the Lowe boy. The rumours are strong – gives him lunch money, buys his books. I've seen them together, a few days ago, under the mango tree, sitting very close, whispering, all very suspicious. All this do-gooding, rubbing the staff the wrong way, is obviously just a ploy to cover up some very dark secrets.

PAT: Man that age, not married, has to be suspicious.

128

CHAPLAIN: Doesn't live anywhere, I gather, half a house, back half. I've been making inquiries, not surprising he can't live some place decent. How can he, when he spends his money procuring? The man has to be stopped, sexually he is a maniac. Let him loose another six months in this school, we'll be having orgies in the Chapel. Such a shame really about the man, potentially a lovely person. What is he doing with his life, eh? What is he accomplishing for himself?

PAT: The point is, what action are we going to take? He must not be allowed to go unchecked.

CHAPLAIN: We have a moral right to society and the school. We have to move quickly, quietly and incisively. This scandal cannot get outside the school. What would people think?

PAT: After all, it's a Church school.

CHAPLAIN: Don't remind me. We will nip it in the bud.

PAT: The Headmaster has to know.

CHAPLAIN: He is well prepared. There has to be an emergency staff meeting at lunch time. Hopal, Joe, you, me, Callender.

PAT: Rosco?

CHAPLAIN: Let's find him. Dacres must have no time to prepare a defence. [*As they prepare to go out*, ROSCO *enters.*] Ah, Mr Callender.

ROSCO: Yes, Bishop?

CHAPLAIN: No time for jokes, man. I suppose you have heard?

ROSCO: No, tell me, nuh?

CHAPLAIN: Serious things are happening in the school, man.

ROSCO: Like what? They shoot the Headmaster?

CHAPLAIN: No such luck, but certain facts have come to light. It's serious! Our mutual friend, Mr Dacres, is not what he makes himself out to be.

ROSCO: Tell me more.

CHAPLAIN: I knew you'd be interested. In fact, the consensus of opinion so far is that he has got to go. Immediate expulsion.

ROSCO: Mr Dacres? Why?

CHAPLAIN: We have to be very hush-hush. The man could wreck the good name of the school. He is infecting the morals of student and staff alike. The man is a sex maniac.

ROSCO: Bishop!

CHAPLAIN: Yes, Mr Callender, we all know this, it is common knowledge. You didn't hear anything?

ROSCO: I have heard one or two rumours, yes, but you know me: I don't listen to rumours or spread gossip. The devil is a wicked man, you know, Bishop: always finds work for idle hands.

MICA: [*Entering*] Where is the Headmaster?

PAT: What's happened, Mica?

MICA: Tell him I have no intention of teaching the dirty little prostitutes in 5B! [*She starts to pack.*] I am going home.

CHAPLAIN: Miss McAdam, what's happened?

MICA: Give me a lift home, Pat.

CHAPLAIN: You can't walk out on us, Miss McAdam.

MICA: You giving me a lift? [*As she is leaving.*]

CHAPLAIN: Mr Campbell, see what you can do. Try and bring her back. That man Dacres is going to wreck the school. [*Enter* JOE.] Mr Josephs, have you seen the Headmaster?

JOE: No.

CHAPLAIN: Serious things are happening. McAdam just walked out. The Headmaster has to be found. [*Exit.*]

ROSCO: You heard any of these rumours, Joe? About Dacres, McAdam and the girl Hermit?

JOE: I have hard rumblings.

ROSCO: Is one of them Pharisees that start the rumours. Jealousy, Joe. Jealousy. Any excuse to get rid of the man. Dacres is an idiot, leave himself wide open. The man is not mi friend, I hold no brief, but is a principle involved. The fellow means well, a little high-handed, but he get plenty benefits for the sufferers in the school. The girl Hermit is no more than another sufferer him trying to help. You people must learn the facts before you jump to conclusions.

JOE: What are the facts?

ROSCO: I see how Dacres operate. Once the Headmaster comes into it, him finish. We have to put in a word for him.

JOE: Excuse me. [*Exit to bathroom.*] Just going to wash my hands.

ROSCO: [*Almost to himself about* JOE] What a little...[*He hisses as the* CHAPLAIN *enters.*]

CHAPLAIN: No sign of the Headmaster. No sign. [*He is going out again as* HENDRY *is entering.*] Ah, Mr Hendry, just the man I wanted to see! Come with me. [HENDRY *is going with the* CHAPLAIN.]

ROSCO: Mr Hendry. [*Calling him back.* HENDRY *twitches as he goes after the* CHAPLAIN.] Come here. [HENDRY *returns as the* CHAPLAIN *re-enters.*]

CHAPLAIN: Hopal, stop wasting time, I'm in a hurry, we have to find the Head.

ROSCO: I feel you people must have some proof before you carry this thing to the Headmaster.

CHAPLAIN: You saw Miss McAdam and the state she was in. The facts speak.

ROSCO: What facts? Rumours!

CHAPLAIN: Come, Mr Hendry. [HENDRY *and the* CHAPLAIN *are going out as* PAT *enters form the opposite direction.*]

Ah, here's Pat. Pat, any luck?

PAT: She's right here.

CHAPLAIN: Good. [PAT *waits by the door for* MICA. *She comes on almost immediately.*] Now tell me what happened?

MICA: It's just too embarrassing.

PAT: It's Dacres and the girl Hermit.

CHAPLAIN: Hermit? Oh yes, you did mention. Who is this girl? I don't know her. What does she look like?

HENDRY: Very tall, black with very big breasts. The students call her 'Hamper'.

CHAPLAIN: Big breasts. I should know her.

HENDRY: It is she they say that take away Mr Dacres from Miss McAdam.

CHAPLAIN: Augh…repeat that.

HENDRY: It is she they say…

CHAPLAIN: I heard you the first time.

PAT: I warned Mica about these rumours, but she thought the best thing was to ignore it. Mica, you better tell them. [*Enter* JOE *from bathroom.*]

MICA: Pat did warn me, but I ignored him. I left for my class and down the corridor I came upon a group of girls laughing, talking and carrying on like dirty little fishwives. I didn't hear what they were saying, but when I passed, there was a sort of hush. No sooner was I a little way off, there was the most disgusting raucous laughter.

CHAPLAIN: Psychological warfare.

MICA: I heard one say…I'm sorry, I won't repeat it. I have no intention of allowing those dirty words to come from my lips.

CHAPLAIN: Oh no!

MICA: I was willing to ignore all that, but I couldn't ignore the lewd, dirty, suggestive drawing that greeted me on the blackboard.

PAT: Captions and all. Tell them about the captions, Mica.

CHAPLAIN: Yes, I would love to hear about these captions. What I would really love to see is the blackboard.

132

PAT: That's erased by now.

CHAPLAIN: The bold, barefaced, vicious, barbaric little sluts! They won't get away with it! Discipline must be maintained at all costs! They'll be expelled! If they get away with it, we can all pack up and leave.

MICA: It's them or me.

CHAPLAIN: They will be dealt with Mica. Of course this situation didn't come about by itself, it was obviously encouraged and nurtured by someone, and that someone, whoever he is, must be punished. That will be the Head's responsibility; but, I am telling you, if he does not take prompt action, I am prepared to go to the Bishop, and there will be hell to pay. This is after all a Church school. We cannot stand back and see fellow teachers subjected to this insulting, disgusting, disgraceful attack. It is humiliating. No, no, Mr Dacres has gone too far.

ROSCO: How Mr Dacres get into this?

CHAPLAIN: Who the hell do you think is responsible?

ROSCO: If you are going to try the man, at least give him a chance to defend himself.

CHAPLAIN: This is not a trial, Mr Callender. For the good of the school, we hope that it would never come to that. Hopefully, he will have the good sense to leave quietly.

ROSCO: How can you, of all people, condemn the man just so?

CHAPLAIN: Condemn him? I don't have to do that. Mr Dacres condemned himself by his actions and his utterances, and the headmaster, who represents the constituted authority in this school, will decide what action must be taken. We mustn't forget, Mr Callender, that the Head himself has been subject to insults and abuses from Mr Dacres. You yourself must have heard the vicious attacks against the constituted authority, and if you say you haven't, I will say you are a liar.

133

ROSCO: The man spoke nothing but the truth. The Headmaster is a shit, and the same goes for all of you.

CHAPLAIN: Now look here!

PAT: Who the hell do you…

MICA: If you think I'm going to stay here and be insulted…

HENDRY: Who do you think you are referring to?

ROSCO: Shut yuh mouth!

HENDRY: Speech is free. If I wish to express myself, I will express myself.

ROSCO: Go in the bathroom and pull the chain!

CHAPLAIN: It doesn't surprise me that a man like you would want to support a man like that. Ten chances to one, you'd do the same thing.

ROSCO: It would be an honour, Bishop, but if anybody was to say I'd follow in your footsteps, now that would be the insult!

CHAPLAIN: I treat you with the contempt you deserve.

ROSCO: And I disregard you.

JOE: Gentlemen, gentlemen. Let's not lose our intentions to petty squabbles and personal clashes. Now I actually haven't heard Mr Dacres attack the Head.

ROSCO: Thank you, Joe.

JOE: I have heard the rumours and I am willing to regard them as rumours.

ROSCO: Thank you, Joe.

JOE: I have no personal axe to grind.

MICA: None of us have.

CHAPLAIN: I don't see this as a personal matter.

PAT: Neither do I. Mr Hendry, do you?

HENDRY: It is not of my nature to bear grudge or carry feelings in my heart for another human being.

JOE: Good. Let's look at the matter objectively. Something bothers me and I must say it.

ROSCO: By all means, Joe.

JOE: As a member of staff who's been here for close on twenty years, my responsibility is to the school.

ROSCO: Hear, hear.

JOE: As teachers, we are dealing with young minds, easily influentiable. We have to be careful how we mould those young minds. [*Pause. No one is certain on whose band wagon* JOE *rides.*] Mr Dacres has been here but for a short time. He has introduced certain things and brought about many changes.

ROSCO: For the better, hear, hear.

JOE: Now I'm all for change…

ROSCO: Hear, hear.

JOE: But change has to be gradual.

CHAPLAIN: Hear, hear.

PAT: Hear, hear.

JOE: Any sudden upheaval must be traumatic.

ROSCO: In fact, Joe, change has to be so slow you never notice it.

JOE: Far from it, but you yourself must have noticed a certain unrest among the students body recently.

CHAPLAIN: A certain tension, yes.

PAT: I've noticed it. The students have been picking on me, calling me names, openly questioning my relevance.

HENDRY: I agree with Pat. I go to my class and I cannot maintain any discipline.

ROSCO: But Hendry, you never could. [HENDRY *picks up a ruler and threatens* ROSCO.]

CHAPLAIN: Gentlemen, let's keep it orderly.

ROSCO: Play with puppy…

CHAPLAIN: Mr Josephs, you were saying?

JOE: Just that the state of unrest in the school was forcibly brought home to me yesterday, when I was approached by a student whose family has a long tradition in this school. This student expressed certain fears and anxieties about the activities of Mr Dacres.

CHAPLAIN: Go on.

JOE: In fact, he went on to suggest that Mr Dacres could be a communist.

CHAPLAIN: Oh my God!

ROSCO: Jesus Christ Joe, how you could say a thing like that?

CHAPLAIN: Hear him out, everybody gets a chance to speak. We must abide by the democratic process.

ROSCO: An intelligent man like you, Joe?

JOE: This student, a thinking student, simply expressed a view.

MICA: That's how the communists operate.

PAT: He's got a following and it's growing.

CHAPLAIN: At the same time, undermining and ridiculing the Head, making a mockery of the constituted authority. Creating disharmony in the staff-room. Contributing to the breakdown of discipline which can only lead to moral decadence and decay. At the same time, preaching racial intolerance, and when he comes in direct conflict with religious, moral and social principles that have served this country well, then I say this man is dangerous.

ROSCO: This is a joke. All you people mad.

CHAPLAIN: Next thing we know it's chaos, confusion, total anarchy. There could be one in every school. Who knows where it could end, unless we put a stop to it now. Now all those in favour of an emergency staff meeting with the Head immediately, say 'Aye'.

[*All except* ROSCO *say* 'Aye'. RUSS *enters. There is a pause.*]

RUSS: I can't get a thing done in my class. The students on all sides of me are running wild. Is this school on holiday?

ROSCO: Now everybody been pressing charges behind the man's back. Right, see the man here, face to face, no more susu.

RUSS: I have a class.

ROSCO: What's happened? Everybody have lockjaw? Mr Hendry?

CHAPLAIN: This is not the time or place.

ROSCO: Come, Mr Hendry. You start the rumours.

HENDRY: I never start no rumours.

ROSCO: Is you I hear with the thing about Dacres and the girl Hermit.

HENDRY: I only repeat what I heard.

RUSS: And what's that, Mr Hendry?

HENDRY: I have nothing to say to you. You hypocrite!

RUSS: I beg your pardon.

HENDRY: Yes. You is a hypocrite, a fraud, a sneaking barefaced fraud, a impostor. Don't ask me about him and the girl Hermit. Ask any of the children in the school. They will tell you. 'bout me start rumour. Look, nuh, man! [*Threatening to fight.*]

PAT: Yes, Mr Dacres, how would you describe your relationship with this girl?

RUSS: I don't have to explain anything to anyone. [*There is a general reaction to his arrogance.*]

MICA: I demand some explanation, Mr Dacres.

RUSS: I'll talk with you Mica, privately.

MICA: It is no longer a private matter, Mr Dacres, not after those disgusting drawings this morning.

HENDRY: I can bear witness to those drawings.

CHAPLAIN: What did they show, Mr Hendry?

HENDRY: A picture of Wilhelmina Hermit with a big stomach, and that man there kissing her and saying, 'Darling, darling', and in the background Miss McAdam is crying and saying, 'It is better to have loved and lost, then never to have loved at all'. That is what I saw.

MICA: Deliberately done to embarrass me!

RUSS: Come now, Mica, you know me well enough. At least you could have come to me directly. I am disappointed.

MICA: I know how I was made to feel.

RUSS: The girls responsible for the smutty drawings are mischief-makers, and should be treated as such. Mica… [*As he takes her away to a quiet corner, the others strain to overhear.*] Wilhelmina boards with an aunt. The aunt's man raped young Wilhelmina. The auntie accused her of trying to take away her man, and threw her out in the streets. Wilhelmina came to me for help when she discovered that she was pregnant. I found her lodgings and…

CHAPLAIN: Who pays for the lodgings?

RUSS: I do.

CHAPLAIN: Oh, so she is still in school and pregnant.

RUSS: She is still in school. [*Pause.*] I took her to a doctor and she had an abortion. [MICA *recoils from him.*]

CHAPLAIN: An abortion, Mr Dacres! [*The others react.* MICA *rests her head on her desk.*]

RUSS: Yes, Reverend Steele. An abortion.

CHAPLAIN: We must admire this Good Samaritan role. You say you paid for this abortion?

RUSS: Partially. Some came from the Welfare Fund.

CHAPLAIN: Just as well I didn't join your welfare society, as if I knew I was going to be party to abortion.

RUSS: What would you have me do? She is only fourteen, Chaplain.

CHAPLAIN: Very laudable, Mr Dacres, but we have to be realistic. You take responsibility for this girl. Does one take such responsibility upon oneself unless one is personally involved? Eh, Mr Campbell? [PAT *laughs nastily.*] Mr Hendry?

HENDRY: You think I born big so?

CHAPLAIN: Mr Josephs?

JOE: It is unbelievable.

CHAPLAIN: Mr Callender, you are a man of the world. Would you shoulder such awesome responsibility without personal involvement?

ROSCO: Don't judge the man by your own standards.

CHAPLAIN: [*To* RUSS] Consider your position, our position, the school's position. This is a Church school. Pray God the Bishop never hears about this. At this point I am not sure if this is a matter for the Board of Governors or the police.

RUSS: My conscience is clear.

CHAPLAIN: But I cannot be a party, Mr Dacres, to any situation where members of staff impute the reputation, my reputation, by being involved in an illegal act. Illegal in the eyes of God and the State. I have no option. I must resign. I will not, and cannot, be a party to it. You have put me in a most untenable position. I resign.

[*General chorus from the rest, except* ROSCO – 'Me too'. *They all start packing up to leave.*]

RUSS: That will not be necessary gentlemen. [*As he collects his things.*] My resignation will be with the Head within the hour. [*The* CHAPLAIN *immediately starts unpacking.*]

CHAPLAIN: I hope you don't see this as a personal matter, Mr Dacres. We have to protect the good name of the school. You may be sure that your good work will be carried on. I will personally look after the welfare myself. We do hope that you will find some success in your new sphere.

[*Exit* RUSS *Down left to the outside.*]

HENDRY: Remember the stench we had here some months aback? It is finally gone. That reminds me, I have a friend, my class-mate, I must ring him and tell him that there is a vacancy here. [*As he goes to the telephone and starts to dial.*]

JOE: [*Quietly*] Oh my God, not another one of them!

CHAPLAIN: Ah Brother Joe, it is a great victory.

HENDRY: [*Leaves the phone and walks across to* JOE.] Brother Joe, you know what really got me about that man, Brother Joe?

JOE: Mr Hendry, don't 'brother Joe' me. I am not your brother, and never will be.

HENDRY: [*He is stung by the retort, but he is no longer the weakling.*] Sticks and stones can break my bones but words cannot hurt me. [*He removes his books, etc. from* JOE's *table, and plonks them down on the main table, sitting in* RUSS DACRES' *chair.*]

CHAPLAIN: Mr Josephs, after all the warmth of fellowship, the harmony of spirit that we shared. [JOE *stares at the* CHAPLAIN, *then sits and readies himself to leave. The* CHAPLAIN *turns to* MICA, *who is crying with head on table.*] This is a tough, hard world, Mica. People disappoint you. My conscience is clear. The matter is closed irrevocably. Now we must deal with the expulsions of the students involved.

ROSCO: How it go, Bishop, the shepherd and the sheep? [*To* JOE] One man let me down. [*As* JOE *goes out.*]

CHAPLAIN: Where were we? Ah yes, students to be expelled. The Head will want my recommendations. [*To* HENDRY] Wilhelmina Hermit? [HENDRY *nods.*] Definitely. The girls responsible for the smutty drawings? [HENDRY *nods.*] Maybe one should temper justice. Long suspensions? [HENDRY *shakes his head.*] No. Discipline must be maintained. [*The bell goes. Exit the* CHAPLAIN *to the Headmaster's door.* HENDRY *stretches, then yawns monstrously.* MICA *looks at him.*]

PAT: Come, Mica. [*Still sobbing, she follows him out.*]
[*The* CHAPLAIN *arrives at the Headmaster's door. He knocks and waits.* HENDRY, *in the staff-room, walks across to* ROSCO's *desk, searches around till he finds a packet of*

cigarettes. ROSCO *walks up to* HENDRY *and watches him.* HENDRY *lights the cigarette in a bold, larger-than-life way, tossing the burnt match on the floor. He blows cigarette smoke in* ROSCO's *face. They face each other threateningly.* ROSCO *turns and walks away;* HENDRY *smiles and strides out arrogantly. The lights fade as music comes up.*]

The Power

Characters

RADIO ANNOUNCER
DAD
TREVOR DAVID
TEACHER
BIRDIE
LAWRENCE
MARK
ISRAEL
THEOPHILUS
CLASS
PRINCESS
TELEGRAM MAN

BBC Radio 5 broadcast The Power in 1992

The Power

A Play For Radio

[*A radio plays an up-tempo version of "Let the Power fall on I". In another room American cartoons play on a television set.*]

RADIO ANNOUNCER: Good morning, Jamaica. The time on your dial is now 7.15, and it is back to school today.

DAD: Come on, Trevor David. Turn off the TV. Trevor David. [*The television set goes off.*]

DAD: We've got half an hour to get to school.

TREVOR DAVID: Ready, Dad.

DAD: Let's go.

[*Sound of a car driving along a fairly busy street.*]

DAD: The traffic's bad.

TREVOR DAVID: You need a car like Night Rider, Dad. Gets you through traffic. Bullet proof. Lazer beam. Computer. Jumps. Talks. Lie detector. You going to miss the light. Speed up, Dad. Missed it. A Night Rider, Dad. That's what you need.

DAD: Yeah. Buy me one.

[*Sound of a car slowing to a halt, and cries of little boys selling newspapers, "Gleaner!", "Herald"!*]

DAD: So, Trevor David. Going to beat the brightest boy in the class this term?

TREVOR DAVID: No, Dad.

DAD: Why not?

TREVOR DAVID: I just can't beat him, Dad.

DAD: What if you worked really hard?

TREVOR DAVID: Daddy, if he's the brightest boy in the class, nobody can beat him.

DAD: Super Boy could beat him.

TREVOR DAVID: Yes, but he's from another planet, Dad. He's got super powers.

DAD: There are people right here on this planet with 'Super' powers.

TREVOR DAVID: Really, Dad?

DAD: Absolutely. In fact there is a story I could tell you about a little boy, round your age, ten, going on eleven, who discovered this quite extraordinary super power.

TREVOR DAVID: He did? Tell me about it Dad.

DAD: Like you, this little boy believed he could never beat the brightest boy in his class.

TREVOR DAVID: So what happened dad? Where did he get the power? What was the source of the power?

DAD: You'll hear. You'll hear. This little boy's name was Theophilus.

TREVOR DAVID: Filofilus.

DAD: No Trevor David - 'THEOPHILUS'. Tongue between the teeth.

TREVOR DAVID: Theophilus.

DAD: That's it. THEOPHILUS. Now, Theophilus lived in a deep rural part of Jamaica, in a little village named "Look Behind". To get to Look Behind, you had to cross seven rivers, over mountains, through valleys. The nearest doctor was twenty miles away so you dare not get sick. Not only was there no doctor in Look Behind, there was no television.

TREVOR DAVID: [*Makes sounds of mock distress.*]

DAD: No radio. No cinema, No electricity, No street lights.

TREVOR DAVID: [*His distress grows.*] Dark days, Daddy.

DAD: If you think those were dark days, then close your eyes. Close them tight. Tight, tight, tight. Really tight. Keep them closed. Even when there was a moon that was what

Look Behind was like at night. Dark. Now, Theophilus lived in a little wattle and daub house.

TREVOR DAVID: What's wattle and daub, Dad?

DAD: A house made of sticks covered with mud.

TREVOR DAVID: Shack.

DAD: More like a mud house, not much bigger than this car. The story of Theophilus, the boy from Look Behind who thought he could never beat the brightest boy in the class, begins on a late afternoon in Look Behind.

[*Sound of knocking on a wooden gate.*]

TEACHER: Hold the dog!

DAD: Everybody had a dog in those days, so whenever you knocked on anybody's gate, you had to call out ...

TEACHER: Hold the dog.

BIRDIE: Dog tie. Come.

TEACHER: Good evening.

BIRDIE: Evening, Sir.

TEACHER: I was hoping to speak to Theophilus's mother or father.

BIRDIE: I am mother and father Sir.

TEACHER: I see. I am Walter McKnight. Theophilus's teacher.

BIRDIE: Delighted to make your acquaintance, Teacher. I am Berdina Johnson. Birdie for short.

TEACHER: Pleased to meet you Miss Birdie. I should have sent a message with Theophilus to say I was coming, but he wasn't in school today. In fact he missed three days this week.

BIRDIE: Sorry about that, Sah, but what with the fact that he don't have no father, he have to help in the field.

TEACHER: His father is dead then, is he?

BIRDIE: No, Sah. Left home one day say he going to town, and has not been seen since.

147

TEACHER: He sends you anything?

BIRDIE: No, Sah. Not even "Howdy", but the Lord will give me strength, and I will find a way. Theophilus not in any sort of trouble is he teacher?

TEACHER: No. No. No nothing of the sort. Quite the opposite in fact. He is a very well behaved boy. A little on the shy side, maybe. Quiet, nice young boy.

BIRDIE: A glad to hear that, Sah. Ahm, I would invite you inside but the house not too ... ahm...

TEACHER: That's all right. What I have to say won't take long. Is Theophilus around ?

BIRDIE: No. He gone fetch water, Sah. Down by the river.

TEACHER: I hear the tank is dry.

BIRDIE: Yes Sah. Is far river we have to go now, but what to do. We need the water.

TEACHER: Miss Birdie. I am here about a very important matter. At this time any child wishing to go to high school has to pay, but as you know most parents don't have the money, so only the privileged can get a secondary education. Recently, the Department of Education made the decision to offer a scholarship open to any boy or girl from a primary school. The scholarship will provide free room and board, books and tuition for a period of five years. Each primary school can enter a candidate. Miss Birdie, I am pleased to inform you, and I am sure that you will be proud to hear, that Theophilus is one of two boys from which the final selection will be made. The finalist will represent Look Behind Primary at the first scholarship exam.

BIRDIE: Theophilus????

TEACHER: Yes.

BIRDIE: You sure you have the name right?

TEACHER: Theophilus Hezekiah Johnson.

BIRDIE: Yes. You have the right name but ... short little boy.
Winjy looking. Black. They call him TAR.

TEACHER: Same one. He could make you very proud.

BIRDIE: I hear what you say, Sah, but, who is the other boy,
Teacher?

TEACHER: Deacon Thompson's son. Mark.

BIRDIE: I know the little boy, Markie well bright. Theophilus
don't stand a chance against the likes of him.

TEACHER: I think it is going to be a tough fight but an equal
fight.

BIRDIE: With due respect Teacher, you wrong this time. The
Thompsons is backra people - people of privilege. We can't
fight them.

TEACHER: You must never let Theophilus hear you say that.

BIRDIE: But is the facts of life, Sah.

TEACHER: No, Miss Birdie. You are wrong. You have to
encourage the boy. Tell him he is the best. Right now
Theophilus' biggest problem is that he has no confidence
in himself, and it shows in his work and that is what you
going have to work on. Building up his confidence. Y'hear
me.

BIRDIE: Yes, Teacher.

TEACHER: You have to help him to believe in himself. And
you will have to believe in him. I will help him, but you
have to do your part.

BIRDIE: Yes Teacher.

TEACHER: All right. I'll come and see you from time to time
to let you know how Theophilus is doing. All right.

BIRDIE: All right, Sah. Walk good.

[TEACHER *walks away, and when he is out of earshot*
BIRDIE *speaks.*]

BIRDIE: Damn fool man.

[*The scene fades and we fade up on three boys, MARK, LAWRENCE and ISRAEL, playing marbles. We hear the sound of the iron marbles as they clink against each other.*]

LAWRENCE: Your play, Mark.

MARK: Watch me now. Going teach you to play marbles, boy. Set me. Nobody beat dat. Ha ha ha.

ISRAEL: You too show off, y'know, Mark. I hope Tar beat you.

MARK: TAR! Beat me? When the time come to take the scholarship, is me going to town.
[*Sounds of marbles.*]
Beat that!

ISRAEL: Hey, who is that I see coming from river with a pan of water on him head? Look like Tar.

LAWRENCE: Is Tar yes.

MARK: Come here, Tar.

ISRAEL: Don't trouble him.

MARK: Boy make teacher beat me today. Watch me an' him.

ISRAEL: It wasn't him.

LAWRENCE: Is him.

ISRAEL: You see you, Lawrence. You too set on.

MARK: Hey! Tar Baby. Tear up batty boy. You don't hear you betters talking to you, enh, jigger-foot boy? How you trousers bottom tear out so? You don't have no more clothes. enh?

LAWRENCE: Is one pants him have. One-pants boy.

MARK: Why you make Teacher beat me?

THEOPHILUS: Move you han' out mi face.

MARK: What happen? You don't like it? Enh. See it here again. Move it if you think you bad.
[*Sound of a slap.*]

150

MARK: You see how the boy chuck me. You want fight. Come.
[*Sounds of blows. Then the sound of the water falling to the ground from Theophilus's head.*]

THEOPHILUS: You see how you make me dash 'way the water. Go back a river for it. If not is me an' you today.
[*Sound of blows.*]

MARK: Lawd, him t'ump me in mi eye.

LAWRENCE: How you mean fi t'ump my friend in him eye, boy. Take dat!

MARK: Hold him, Lawrence. Let me teach him a lesson.
[*Sound of blows.*]
Say you a run competition 'gainst me. You is a lower class boy. You must know your place.
[*Sound of blows.*]

TEACHER: [*Calling from off mike*] Hey, you boys. Mark. Lawrence. Stop the fighting.

ISRAEL: TEACHER!

TEACHER: Stop it, I said.

ISRAEL: Is teacher. Run.

MARK: Pick up the marbles. Pick up the marbles an' come.
[MARK, ISRAEL *and* LAWRENCE *run off as* TEACHER MCNIGHT *approaches.*]

TEACHER: You stay right there, Theophilus. You mother send you to the river and you out here fighting.

THEOPHILUS: Is dem trouble me, teacher.

TEACHER: That is the water your mother sent you for, boy?

THEOPHILUS: Is dem pitch it off mi head, Teacher.

TEACHER: I will deal with them tomorrow. Where you going to get water now to carry home to your mother, boy?

THEOPHILUS: Me have to go back to river, Sir.

TEACHER: At this hour of the evening! You don't see night coming? I tell you what. Come with me.

151

[The scene fades and there is a short bridge of Jamaican period music, then we segue into sounds of the night. Crickets, toads, frogs etc. TEACHER MCKNIGHT and THEO-PHILUS walk along the dark and lonely country track. In the distance we hear the up-tempo singing of a Revival song, accompanied by tambourines.]

TEACHER: It's got so dark, so quickly. So Theophilus..

THEOPHILUS: Yes, Teacher.

TEACHER: You have to come to school every day from now on.

THEOPHILUS: I will try Teacher.

TEACHER: Try. You have to do more than that. It's a must. No more going to river for water. 'Tween now and when we decide between you an Mark, you can come to my house for water. You going have to buckle down an do some serious work. Come let us cut through this church yard an..

THEOPHILUS: No, Teacher. No.

TEACHER: Where you going so fast? Come back here Theophilus, wait for me. If we go through the church yard, it'll cut off half the distance.

THEOPHILUS: Can't go through there Sir.

TEACHER: Why not? Slow down Theophilus. Come give me your hand. You are as cold as ice. Why is your pulse racing so fast? What scared you so? Why you stopped? Come on. Theophilus.

THEOPHILUS: WWWWWWWhat's dat ?

TEACHER: Where ?

THEOPHILUS: UUUUUUp ahead.

TEACHER: A banana leaf. What you thought it was?

THEOPHILUS: Ahm. Ahm..

TEACHER: It's alright. No need to be afraid. What you so scared of Theophilus? Come on. Tell me.

152

THEOPHILUS: Is... Is... Is the preacher at the church Sir.

TEACHER: Why you so afraid of him?

THEOPHILUS: Everybody 'fraid him.

TEACHER: But why?

THEOPHILUS: The preacher is a man with powers, Teacher.

TEACHER: POWERS!!!!!!

THEOPHILUS: Yes Teacher. He can set evil spirit on you. Turn you wrong side. Send you to mad house or even worse dan dat. He can do anything. See into the future... Look into the past. People come from far an near to see him. Some very backra people to Sir.

TEACHER: Is alright. Just hold my hand. No need to be afraid.

[*The singing from the church gets louder and the scene fades, and we fade up on the interior of "Look Behind Primary School. 'The school', a cramped open space affair, is in session. We can imagine nine classes with approximately fifty students per class. Concentration is on the three 'Rs' with a smattering of geography, literature, simple science and civics. The learning is mostly by rote, each class desperately trying to hear themselves over the next. Corporal punishment is administered freely. The school bell goes.*]

TEACHER: Everybody stand. And ah...Mark and Theophilus don't forget that you are to stay behind for extra lessons. Close your eyes class. Our father who art in heaven ... [*The scene fades and there is quiet.*]

TEACHER: Now, I have the marks for the last test. Where are they? Ah here we are. English Language Comprehension. Not bad at all, Mark. Very good, in fact, apart from one or two careless mistakes. The plural of 'story' is.....

MARK: 'Stories', Teacher.

TEACHER: Yes, but how you spell stories?

MARK: S T O R Y I...

TEACHER: Nonsense. Nonsense. Think again.

MARK: S T O R I E S, Sir.

TEACHER: That is correct. Careless, careless. Make a silly mistake like that. Otherwise very good. You got ninety eight.

MARK: Aieee.

TEACHER: Theophilus.

THEOPHILUS: Yes Teacher.

TEACHER: Mary is the taller or tallest of the three girls. Which is correct?

MARK: Me teacher. Me teacher.

TEACHER: Quiet Mark. Theophilus.

[*Pause*]

TEACHER: Why you looking so frightened? I am not going to eat you.

MARK: Tallest Teacher.

TEACHER: Tallest. Theophilus. Tallest. You were not here when I was doing this so I will have to go over it with you. You didn't do badly all the same. Ninety three.

MARK: Beat you. Street an' lane. Ride him jockey…

TEACHER: Quiet, Mark. In the maths however, congratulations Theophilus, you got full marks, 100%, and Mark, 97%.

MARK: What I get wrong Teacher?

TEACHER: There is the paper. Look at it. In science, Mark you got 96%, Theophilus 94%.

MARK: Beat you again.

TEACHER: Now, for today's work. Turn to page four in your Royal Reader. Excuse me a minute boys, I'll be right back.

MARK: You feel good, how you beat me in the arithmetic.

THEOPHILUS: Feel good yes.

MARK: You never really beat me y'know.

THEOPHILUS: I beat you.

MARK: I deliberately get one wrong to give you a little encouragement. I feel sorry for you. I was just toying with you. You really think you did beat me? You gone crazy or what? No man. I can beat you any time I want, you know that. You is my beating stick. As long as you live you will never beat me. Learn that.

[*The scene fades and when we fade up again we are at the exterior of Miss Birdie's little wattle and daub house. We hear birds twittering and the pig squealing.*]

THEOPHILUS: Evening Mama.

BIRDIE: Is now you coming from school?

THEOPHILUS: Teacher keep me in for extra lessons.

BIRDIE: You an dis damn scholarship. How you got on today?

THEOPHILUS: Not so good Mama.

BIRDIE: Mark beat you in all three subject again?

THEOPHILUS: Yes Mama.

BIRDIE: But you tell me you did so well in the 'Rithmetic.

THEOPHILUS: Didn't beat him Mama.

BIRDIE: As I expected son. No way you can beat the likes of him so don't fret yourself. Ferget 'bout the scholarship. An you can forget school tomorrow.

THEOPHILUS: I don't want to go either Mama, but Teacher say...

BIRDIE: I don't give a damn what Teacher say. Teacher don't rule here. Saturday is market day and not a thing prepare. So you have to stay home tomorrow an help me. The yam have to dig. Me alone can't dig it, then carry it up to the yard and the banana have to cut. As well there is three nice breadfruit on the tree. So ferget 'bout school tomorrow my friend.

THEOPHILUS: O.K Mama

[*Thunder rolls in the distance.*]

BIRDIE: Sound like rain. I hope it come. The time so dry.

[*The pig squeals again.*]

BIRDIE: The pig get away so come an help me catch him. Him in dat little bush behind the orange tree. You go so and I go di other way.

THEOPHILUS: Give me the rope Mama.

BIRDIE: See it here.

THEOPHILUS: Easy now. Easy.

[*There is a kerfuffle and the pig squeaks.*]

BIRDIE: Lie down on him.

THEOPHILUS: Me get him Mama. Me get him.

[*The thunder rolls again. The scene fades and when we fade up again the rain is bucketing down. The lightning flashes and the thunder rolls.*]

THEOPHILUS: Is really a nice shower Mama.

BIRDIE: We needed it Son.

[*The rain now starts bucketing down on the thatch roof.*]

BIRDIE: Like it really out to come.

[*A flash of lightning followed by thunder.*]

BIRDIE: Lord of mercy. Lord of mercy

THEOPHILUS: Lord of Mercy, Christ of Mercy.

BIRDIE: Where you gone? Come from under the bed Man. Big boy like you 'fraid a lightning.

THEOPHILUS: It getting closer and closer every time, you know Mama.

BIRDIE: Don't fret your self. Lightning never strike at night.

THEOPHILUS: Lightning can strike any time Mama.

BIRDIE: Where you get that nonsense from?

THEOPHILUS: Is a fact mama. Teacher say that....

BIRDIE: Foolishness. From I was a little girl I hear that lightning don't strike at night, so I don't know what you teacher coming with. Don't believe a word he tell you.

THEOPHILUS: Mama. Listen. Dat sound.

BIRDIE: What?

THEOPHILUS: The bed wetting up.

BIRDIE: Get the wash pan. Set it on the bed. Months now that man promise to fix the roof. Look how long now the thatch throw down out side. We going soak bad tonight. Take up your book an you school uniform boy. Quick.

THEOPHILUS: Alright Mama. Alright. Where me must put them?

BIRDIE: Put them under the Mattress. Lord of mercy as you set a container, another place start to leak.

THEOPHILUS: Mama, we don't have anything else leave to catch water, and the whole roof look like it going to collapse.

BIRDIE: Lord help us.

THEOPHILUS: Mama, A soon come.

BIRDIE: Where you going?

THEOPHILUS: See if me can cover the roof with some of the thatch, Mama.

BIRDIE: You can't go out there now.

THEOPHILUS: Mama. [*As he opens the door and goes out into the rain*] Me have to try an' do something.

BIRDIE: Come back. Come back. It too dangerous. Next thing you know you roll off di roof an bruck you neck.

THEOPHILUS: Is alright Mama. Get the broom an poke it up in the roof, an tell me where is the worse place.

BIRDIE: Where you is? I can't see you.

THEOPHILUS: I climbing the mango tree so I can swing across to the roof.

[*A really loud bolt of lightning, followed by monstrous roll of thunder.*]

BIRDIE: Lord of Mercy. Lord of Mercy. Theophilus. Theophilus. Theophilus.

THEOPHILUS: Yes Mama.

BIRDIE: You alright?

THEOPHILUS: Yes Mama. Mama. Mama look. A ball of fire in the sky. Lightning strike the coconut tree.

BIRDIE: Lord of his mercy. Come down. Come down NOW.

[*We fade the effects of the rain and it fades up again a few moments later. Theophilus and Birdie are again in the little room.*]

THEOPHILUS: Like the rain don't look like it out to ease up at all tonight Mama.

BIRDIE: Is alright man. It can fall all it like now. Not even one leak. Not one. You worth yuh weight in gold you know little boy. You is God's gift to a mother.

[*Theophilus sort of gives a shy little laugh. Fade, then the rooster crows in the distance.*]

BIRDIE: Daylight already? Thank you Lord for a good night sleep, an t'ank you for the rain, an Lord, A can't get over how lightning strike the coconut tree last night. You send me a sign or what? Is a sign? What you trying to tell me Lord. Hmm. I wonder...Theophilus. Theophilus.

THEOPHILUS: Hmmm.

BIRDIE: Wake up.

THEOPHILUS: Time is it Mama ?

BIRDIE: Second cock just crow. That should make it about six o'clock, but what with all that rain last night. I think even the rooster sleep late. Time to get up an'get ready for school.

THEOPHILUS: But Mama, you ferget dat you tell me...

BIRDIE: The tank full. No need to go to river for water...

THEOPHILUS: But other things to do Mama.

BIRDIE: You heard what I just said.

THEOPHILUS: Yes Mama.

BIRDIE: Well then, just do as I tell you before A change mi mind.

[*The scene fades as the cock crows and we fade up on Look Behind Primary in session. It is assembly time*]

TEACHER: Good morning children.

PUPILS: Good morning Teacher.

TEACHER: On this day, May 24th, Empire Day, we celebrate the birthday of our beloved Queen. Let us all stand and wish her a happy birthday.

PUPILS: Happy birthday Queen Victoria. Thank you for the penny and thank you for the bun.

TEACHER: Now let us all wave our red white and blue flags and sing....Rule Britannia

[*The children join in and sing the song...After a few bars we fade and the focus switches to Teacher Mc Knight's class.*]

TEACHER: Pay attention class. Question number five. What year did Christopher Columbus discover Jamaica? Hands up.

[*The hands go up, much flicking of the fingers.*]

PUPILS: Me teacher. Me teacher. Me teacher.

TEACHER: Let's see who doesn't have their hand up. Theophilus. You must know the answer to that question. Let me hear you. Come on Theophilus. Come on. Come on. [*Teacher McKnight is beginning to put serious pressure on Theophilus.*]

THEOPHILUS: Seventeen, seventeen...

TEACHER: Seventeen seventeen???

159

[*There is much laughter from the pupils as they continue to shout. "Me Teacher" all the while the hands up and flicking.*]

TEACHER: It is not funny. Nonsense. Mark.

MARK: 1492 Teacher.

TEACHER: Very good Mark. What's happening to you Theophilus? Look like you want a little waking up. I have Mr. Right all things wrong with me. Soaked him in oil last night so he should be stinging like a scorpion today. Let's see who will be the first to feel Mr. Right today. Question number six. Kingston is now the capital of Jamaica. Where was the capital before?

[*Again the thrust of hands into the air and the flicking of the fingers, and "Me Teacher"*]

TEACHER: Theophilus.

THEOPHILUS: Port Royal Teacher.

[*The class breaks into laughter.*]

TEACHER: What. Come here to me, and hold out your hand. [*Sound of the strap hitting Theophilus' hand. Theophilus remains silent during the beating.*]

TEACHER: Mr. Right don't seem to me having much effect on you today. Look like I will have to change the medicine. Somebody go and cut me a guava switch.

[*Sound of a hand held school bell ringing.*]

TEACHER: Saved by the bell, Theophilus. See me after school.

[*The scene fades as the students stream out of class for the recess period. We fade up again a little while later in the classroom.*]

TEACHER: Theophilus. Come. Talk to me. What's the problem?

THEOPHILUS: Nothing, Teacher.

TEACHER: I don't understand. The extra lessons don't seem to be helping you at all. Like you was doing better when you came to school two or three days a week. Give your mother her due she hasn't stopped you once in weeks. Instead of getting better you getting worse. The test to decide 'tween you an Mark is next Thursday. I don't know what to do. I beat you. I cane you. Mark is streaks ahead of you. And you can do better work than him. You have the ability. I know you can beat him.

THEOPHILUS: Can't beat him Teacher.

TEACHER: Why not?

THEOPHILUS: Him is the brightest boy in the class.

TEACHER: Why you keep telling yourself that? It's not true.

THEOPHILUS: Is true, Teacher.

TEACHER: If you keep telling yourself that you will never beat him. You have to think positive, and believe in yourself and in your ability. You are a bright boy. And this is a chance in a lifetime. Think what it would mean Theophilus. High School. Then a nice job. The chance to help your mother. Buy her a nice house with a tank. That would make her happy.

THEOPHILUS: Yes Sir, but I can't beat Mark, Sir.

TEACHER: [*Beat*] Tell you what. Let's go for a little walk.

[*The scene fades and when we fade up again we hear birds twittering in open country.*]

TEACHER: That is a beautiful little bird. Isn't it pretty?

THEOPHILUS: Yes, Sir.

TEACHER: What bird is it you know?

THEOPHILUS: Is a Banana Katie, Sir. Live in the Banana Tree.

TEACHER: Nature is wonderful, isn't it? All those different
   birds, different colours. What's that one? Listen.
   [*Sound of a woodpecker, pecking away.*]
THEOPHILUS: The woodpecker. See him there, Teacher.
TEACHER: Where?
THEOPHILUS: On the coconut tree. Making a nest.
TEACHER: Isn't it amazing Theophilus, that little bird with
   that little beak trying to bore a hole into the trunk of that
   really tough tree. Peck, peck, pecking away.
   [*Sound continues of woodpecker pecking at the tree.*]
TEACHER: Must have a lot of patience and confidence in
   himself to tackle an impossible job like that. And he never
   fails does he?
THEOPHILUS: No Teacher.
TEACHER: [*To himself*] I guess I'll just have to keep pecking away.
   [*In the distance we hear an up-tempo revival song coming
   from the Revivalist church.*]
SONG Oh let the power fall on me,
   Let the power fall on me,
   O let the power from Zion fall on me,
   Oh let the power fall on me etc.
TEACHER: [*Hums along with the singing in the distance.*]
   I guess the only thing left for me to do now Theophilus is to
   go see the preacher man with the power. Why you look at
   me so? Maybe he could help. What you think? Think he
   could help you beat Mark?
THEOPHILUS: Yes Teacher.
TEACHER: You really believe he could help you?
THEOPHILUS: Yes, Teacher.
TEACHER: Why not? In fact Theophilus, come to think of it I
   know of another man who has got ten, umpteen times more
   power than the preacher man. This man can make you fly
   through the air, sail under the sea. He's got extraordinary

162

powers. Let me discuss it with Miss Birdie and if she agrees, I will go and see him for you. Of course you realise this has to be a secret between us.

THEOPHILUS: Yes teacher.

[*The scene fades and when we fade up again we are inside the schoolroom of Look Behind Primary.*]

TEACHER: Good morning class.

PUPILS: Good morning teacher.

TEACHER: This morning we have Science. Let me here you spell the word "SCIENCE"

PUPILS: S C I E N C E.

TEACHER: Very good. Now today we are going to conduct a little experiment. As you can see on my desk I have two jam jars filled with ...What does it look like to you?

PUPILS: Water teacher.

TEACHER: Now, I would like two volunteers to come up to my desk.

PUPILS: Me Teacher, Me Teacher!

TEACHER: Who shall we have? Princess and Theophilus. Come. Now hold out your hands. Turn them over. Now the rest of the class gather round. Very good. Not too close. I want every body to be able to see.

TEACHER: Now class I want you to watch carefully. I am going to pour a little of the liquid on the back of Princess' hand. There we are. Now Princess I want you to very gently blow on the water. [*Princess blows on the water*] Again.

PRINCESS: Nothing happen Sir.

TEACHER: Now I am going to pour from this jar. Hold your hand properly, Theophilus. There we are. Now Theophilus, I want you to blow very gently. Now.

[*Theophilus blows.*]

THEOPHILUS: It disappear. It just disappear. An' mi hand feel cool.

[*There is much excitement from the onlookers. "It disappear",* *"Yes" "Where it went, Teacher?", "How it do that?", "Do it on* *my hand, Teacher", "Is Magic". A chorus of "Do it on my* *hand, Teacher."*]

THEOPHILUS: Mi hand still feel cool. Is magic.

TEACHER: Not quite. If I can explain? What happens when you put a pot filled with water on a fire and leave it. Mark?

MARK: If you leave it long enough it would boil up Teacher.

TEACHER: And after a while if you didn't take the pot off the fire. What would happen? Israel?

ISRAEL: The water would boil out Sir.

TEACHER: And what would you see coming out of the pot? Theophilus?

THEOPHILUS: Steam, Teacher.

TEACHER: Very good. Now can anyone in this class tell me what is the word that describes what happens when you apply heat to water and it turns to steam or gas? Does anybody know? I will give you a clue. It begins with E and ends with N.

MARK: Evaporation, Sir.

TEACHER: Very, very good Mark. What is the word class?

PUPILS: Evaporation, Teacher.

TEACHER: Now all liquids will boil depending on how much heat you put to them. Some need lots of heat and others need very little heat. In this jar, the one I put on your hand, Princess, is water. Pure and simple. In this other jar, the one I put on your hand, Theophilus, is a liquid that looks like water, but is in fact not water. It is methyl alcohol, commonly called methylated spirit. Now methylated spirit has a low boiling point. When you blew on it, Theophilus, you blew out hot air and that was enough heat to change it from

164

liquid to gas. It happened so quickly you could feel it but you could not see it. Next week we will look at the opposite of evaporation......

[*The scene fades and we fade up again to hear a knocking on a wooden gate.*]

TEACHER: Hold dog.

BIRDIE: Come Teacher.

TEACHER: Miss Birdie. How are you?

BIRDIE: Give God thanks, Sah. An' you,Teacher?

TEACHER: Very well thank you Miss Birdie.

BIRDIE: [*She calls*] Theophilus. Teacher is here.

THEOPHILUS: Coming Mama.

BIRDIE: Come this way Teacher, an watch you step Sah. The house is very humble as you can see.

TEACHER: Miss Birdie, when I was a little boy I lived in a house no bigger than this. Dirt floor, wattle and daub. Same thing. I am from a very humble background and I am not ashamed of it.

THEOPHILUS: Evening, Teacher.

TEACHER: Evening, Theophilus. Come in and close the door so we can get down to business. I can sit on the bed.

BIRDIE: Go right ahead, Teacher.

TEACHER: Now, as I promised I went to town and I saw the man with the extraordinary powers and I explained the situation to him and he said he would be willing to help. He can't guarantee that Theophilus will win the scholarship. All he can promise is that Theophilus will perform to the best of his abilities. And I tell you one thing Miss Birdie, if Theophilus performs as I know he can then I think we have a winner. Now he gave me this pouch. Take it. Look at it. Pass it to Theophilus. Thank you Theophilus. Now inside

165

of the pouch. I am going to open it very carefully, and in it are these four vials. Each filled with a different oil. Read for me please Theophilus.

THEOPHILUS: [*Reading the labels on the vials.*] Oil of Success. Oil of I believe in myself. Oil of Self Confidence. Oil of determination.

TEACHER: Now I am going to put them back in the pouch. Keep it under your pillow. First thing in the morning and last thing at night before you go to bed you must hold the pouch. Cup it in your hand like this and say quietly to yourself "I got the power in my hands". Say it over and over. When ever you come up against a problem, what do you say?

THEOPHILUS: I got the power in my hands.

TEACHER: These are good powers. You have nothing to fear. Once a week every Thursday at sunset, you must open the pouch and hold the vials up to the evening sun. Then you must return the vials to the pouch, then put it back under your pillow. On the day of the exam, you must take the pouch with you. Let me hear what you say?

THEOPHILUS: I got the power in my hands.

[*The scene fades. Then there is the sound of a cock crowing.*]

THEOPHILUS: I got the power in my hands.

[*Sound of the school bell ringing… Children pouring out of school. Then the sound of a small river running freely. Sound of clothes being washed in the river.*]

BIRDIE: Lord, see me poor sinner down here by your river washing these clothes. I getting tired Lord. Give me the strength to go on an Lord like David against Goliath. Is Theophilus against Mark today. I know Theophilus got the power to do his best, but when I think Lord that if Theophilus come out the winner den I going have to buy him shoes an clothes to wear to town to take the scholarship an when I t'ink Lord of all the other things I could do with the money.

Strengthen my faith Lord......

[*Above the roar of the river, we hear Theophilus calling from over the hill.*]

THEOPHILUS: Mama. Mama. [*His voice echoes through the valley.*]

BIRDIE: Come. Come. Me down by the river.

THEOPHILUS: [*Getting closer*] Mama, Mama. Guess what!!!!

BIRDIE: Come. Come.

THEOPHILUS: Mama. Mama. I beat him. I beat him. I beat the brightest boy in the class.

BIRDIE: Hallelujah. Thank you Lord. Thank you. First thing tomorrow A going get him them shoes an what ever else him need.

THEOPHILUS: You heard me Mama.

BIRDIE: The power working, son.

THEOPHILUS: Yes Mama, it working.

[*Sound of the school bell ringing. The bell quietens all activity and the teacher calls the school to order.*]

TEACHER: Good afternoon children.

PUPILS: Good afternoon Teacher.

TEACHER: Tomorrow is the big day when Theophilus journeys to Kingston to do the scholarship exam. He will be up against the brightest boys and girls from all over Jamaica. All that is left for me to say to you Theophilus is, do your best. Go with determination and confidence and remember you have the power in your hands. Don't forget; be at my house before first cock crow ready to travel.

[*Birdie sings a little song. "Power, Power, Power. He's got the power in his hands. Glory Hallelujah. Oh what a power in his hands." etc. Sound of the cock crowing in the distance. Miss Birdie stirs...*]

BIRDIE: What's dat? Third cock crow. That should put it at about half past six. The hour that little boy leave here this

167

morning. Wonder where him reach? Could all be in town by now. Hmm. What an excitement in mi life if him win. Can't win. Can't lose with The Power. It would be a wonderful t'ing. Theophilus H. Johnson, Scholarship winner. [*She laughs quietly and pleasurably.*] High school. Few years time big job. White shirt and tie. Can just see him. Don't even bother think 'bout it...Get up. Wonder what time it is in truth? Hmm. First thing I would ask him to buy for me is a time piece. What a t'ing- see me a tell time. Would have to learn to read it first. Dat would be the problem...Get up, and tidy the house. Alright, the little boy throw him clothes all over the....Lord of Mercy. Theophilus forget the pouch. Lord of Mercy. Lord of Mercy. Oh Lord. Oh Lord. Oh Lord. Woi. [*A cry of pain*] Woi.

[*Urban Sounds. The sound of the tram car going by. Motor vehicles. Urban street cries. Children leaving the exam.*]

TEACHER: Theophilus. Theophilus. Over here. How was the exam?

THEOPHILUS: Think I did well Teacher.

BIRDIE: [*calling from Off*] Teacher. Teacher.

THEOPHILUS: Mama.

TEACHER: Miss Birdie. What you doing in town ?

BIRDIE: The exam finish?

TEACHER: Just over.

BIRDIE: Lord of his mercy.

THEOPHILUS: What happened Mama?

BIRDIE: Oh Lord. Oh Lord. Oh Lord.

TEACHER: What is the problem Miss Birdie?

BIRDIE: Theophilus forget the pouch.

TEACHER: THEOPHILUS.

THEOPHILUS: I didn't need it Teacher.

BIRDIE: WHAT!!! After I move heaven and earth to bring it for you. What you mean you didn't need it? TEACHER?

TEACHER: THEOPHILUS ?

THEOPHILUS: Teacher trick me Mama.

BIRDIE: Trick you. What you mean trick you?

THEOPHILUS: I follow your instructions as you said, Teacher, but last Thursday when I open the pouch, the vials were empty.

BIRDIE: EMPTY?

THEOPHILUS: Yes Mama… They was as dry as chip. I examine the pouch. No sign of anything leak out. No stain. They look as if they been dry for days. I start to panic but then I remember: that same Thursday I got one hundred in Arithmetic. So I put my brain to work Mama. Maybe I got the hundred on my own. I didn't say anything to anybody. Next day I got ninety nine in science and a hundred in civics. A thought come to me. Dat evening I examine the vials. Look closely Mama.

BIRDIE: A little hole in all of them. But even if the oil leak out, it should be in the pouch.

THEOPHILUS: Methylated spirit Mama.

BIRDIE: Methy what?

THEOPHILUS: It evaporates Mama. Teacher trick me Mama.

BIRDIE: Teacher?

TEACHER: Theophilus is right Miss Birdie. When I saw the exam approaching and his work was getting from bad to worse. I knew what the problem was. No confidence in himself and in his abilities. I had to try something. I am proud of you son. Come on let's go home and await the results. Win or lose he did it on his own.

[*The scene fades and we return to the present.*]

DAD: So that's it Trevor David. The story of Theophilus the boy who found the source of the ultimate power. Where?

TREVOR DAVID: Within himself Dad. I get it. The power is within you. Wicked story Dad. Wicked. But what happened Dad? Did Theophilus win the scholarship?

DAD: For the answer to that question Trevor David, we have to return to the little village of Look Behind, on one of the darkest nights of the year.

[The scene fades and we return to the village of Look Behind. A dog barks in the night. Sound of knocking on a wooden gate.]

MALE VOICE: Hold dog.

BIRDIE: Theophilus. Wake up.

THEOPHILUS: [*Half asleep*] Yes, Mama.

BIRDIE: Listen.

MALE VOICE: Hold dog.

BIRDIE: Who could dat be at dis hour? Coming. Light the lamp, Theophilus. A coming. A coming.

[Birdie opens the door.]

BIRDIE: Who dat?

MALE VOICE: Telegram for Miss Berdina Johnson.

BIRDIE: Sign for it Theophilus. What calamity is dis now in mi life?

MALE VOICE: Sign right here little boy.

BIRDIE: [*Muttering to herself.*] Bad news. I know is bad news. Somebody dead.

MALE VOICE: That's it. Here you is little boy. Night.

BIRDIE / THEOPHILUS: Night.

THEOPHILUS: Open it, Mama?

BIRDIE: No.

THEOPHILUS: But Mama...

BIRDIE: Alright, but open it slow.

[Theophilus tears it open fast.]

BIRDIE: Slow, A said. What it say?

THEOPHILUS: [*Reading*] We are pleased to inform you that....
Mama, A win the scholarship.. Mama..Mama.
[*Birdie begins to cry.*]

BIRDIE: Son. Son. Hug me tight. Tight. Tight. Thank you
Jesus. Aye. Hey Teacher don't know. He going be so happy.
Come A going just so...

[*The scene fades and as we fade up again we hear Theophilus
and Birdie running up the road towards the teacher's house.
Birdie continues to offer praises to the Lord. Up ahead we
hear the up-tempo singing of the revivalist song "I got the
power" coming from the revivalist church.*]

THEOPHILUS: Come Mama, we can cut through the
church.

BIRDIE: You mad or what?

THEOPHILUS: Nothing to be afraid of Mama. Come.

BIRDIE: No.

THEOPHILUS: Is alright. Mama. I got the greater power now.
Come hold mi hand Mama. That's it. Come. Come.
[*The singing from the revivalist church gets louder and
louder.*]

THEOPHILUS: Teacher going be so proud of me.

BIRDIE: Yes son. Yes.

[*The singing builds and then fades.*]

The End
August 1992

Glossary

A	I (remains as 'I' when used for emphasis)
ackee and saltfish	a Jamaican dish
backra	white
Bellevue	the name of a mental asylum
blouse beat!	an expression of surprise
blue drawers	a Jamaican dish
bruck	broken
buss	burst
bwoy	boy
battyman	homosexual
cheups	a light affectionate kiss on the lips
'coz	because
cuss	curse
dass	that's
dat	that
dem	them
dis	this
F.I.U.	Financial Intelligence Unit – a unit for policing the leakage of foreign exchange
gal	girl
ginny	jenny-ass, female donkey
hear dey	listen to that
mi	my
mi nuh 'fraid	I am not afraid
nah Sah	no sir
nutten	nothing
odder	other
out dey	out there, outside

pickney	child
riddim	rhythm
sah	sir
Star	Jamaican evening newspaper
tief	steal
wid	with
yampi	yam
yuh	your (when used as an adjective: e.g., "yuh head") you (when used as a pronoun: e.g., "where yuh going")

Macmillan Caribbean Writers

Series Editor: Jonathan Morley

Look out for other exciting titles from the region:

Crime thrillers:

Rum Justice: *Jolien Harmsen*

Fiction:

The Girl with the Golden Shoes: *Colin Channer*
The Festival of San Joaquin: *Zee Edgell*
She's Gone: *Kwame Dawes*
Molly and the Muslim Stick: *David Dabydeen*
John Crow's Devil: *Marlon James*
This Body: *Tessa McWatt*
Walking: *Joanne Haynes*
Trouble Tree: *John Hill Porter*
Power Game: *Perry Henzell*
For Nothing At All: *Garfield Ellis*
Brother Man: *Roger Mais*
The Humming-Bird Tree: *Ian McDonald*

Short Stories:

Fear of Stones: *Kei Miller*
(shortlisted for the 2007 Commonwealth Writers' Prize)

Poetry:

Poems of Martin Carter: *Stewart Brown and Ian McDonald (eds.)*
Selected Poems of Ian McDonald: *Edward Baugh (ed.)*

Plays:

Bellas Gate Boy (includes audio CD): *Trevor D Rhone*